THE
STOKE CITY
MISCELLANY

For Mark Chamberlain and Peter Beagrie – two of the finest wingers I was lucky enough to see

THE
STOKE CITY
MISCELLANY

DAVID CLAYTON

The
History
Press

First published 2009
This new edition in paperback first published in 2012

The History Press
The Mill, Brimscombe Port
Stroud, Gloucestershire, GL5 2QG
www.thehistorypress.co.uk

British Library Cataloguing in Publication Data.
A catalogue record for this book is available from the British
Library.

ISBN 978 0 7524 8629 1

Typesetting and origination by The History Press
Printed in Great Britain by CMP (uk) Limited

ACKNOWLEDGEMENTS

Thanks to all the Stoke City fans who helped me during the research of this book and thanks also to Michelle Tilling, my editor at The History Press, Will Unwin, Alexander Rowen, Luke McDowall and special thanks, as always, to my wife Sarah and our three beautiful young children, Harry, Jaime and Chrissie. That's pretty much it – for facts and figures from elsewhere, thanks as well. You know who you are.

David Clayton, 2012

WHAT BETTER WAY TO START THAN WITH THE LYRICS TO . . .

Delilah

I saw the light on the night that I passed by her window
I saw the flickering shadows of love on her blind
She was my woman
As she deceived me I watched and went out of my mind
My, my, my, Delilah
Why, why, why, Delilah?
I could see that girl was no good for me
But I was lost like a slave that no man could free

At break of day when that man drove away, I was
    waiting
I crossed the street to her house and she opened the
    door
She stood there laughing
I felt the knife in my hand and she laughed no more
My, my, my Delilah
Why, why, why Delilah?
So before they come to break down the door
Forgive me Delilah, I just couldn't take any more

She stood there laughing
I felt the knife in my hand and she laughed no more
My, my, my, Delilah
Why, why, why, Delilah?
So before they come to break down the door
Forgive me Delilah, I just couldn't take any more
Forgive me Delilah, I just couldn't take any more

AND WHILE WE'RE SINGING ...

Here are some of City's favourite chants and songs – at least the printable ones!

We are the Potters, the rip-roaring Potters, back in the Prem where Pulis got us, so come on everybody let's keep Stoke up, keep Stoke up, keep Stoke up!

Who would have believed Slim Shady himself, Eminem, wrote that?

He dives like a tart,
he cries like a kid,
your boy Ronaldo,
loves Real Madrid.

Stoke fans serenade the Madrid-bound Manchester United midfielder during a trip to Old Trafford

Don't you wish your striker was James Beattie?
Don'tcha? Don'tcha?
Don't you wish your striker was James Beattie?
Don'tcha? Don'tcha?

The Potters' fans again show their ability to turn the tune of the day (this time it was a Pussycat Dolls hit) into a terrace classic

Who needs Robinho?
We've got Delap's throw.

An equally lethal weapon when all the assists are counted up

One F in Fuller,
There's only one F in Fuller!

A clever way round the expletives?

City . . . City . . . tell the boys in red and white
everything will be alright
City . . . City . . . you're the pride and joy of us today
We'll be with you, be with you, be with you every step
along the way
We'll be with you, be with you, be with you, be by your
side we'll always stay.
Stoke it up!

Feed the Beast and he will score,
Feed the Beast, Feed the Beast,
Feed the Beast and he will score,
Feed the Beast and he will score!

An ode to Jon 'The Beast' Parkin

YOU CAN'T CALL ME AL

Former Stoke City boss Alan A'Court had two nasty
brushes with non-League sides during his career. The
former Liverpool and England stalwart was playing for
Liverpool when Worcester City caused one of the all-
time biggest FA Cup shocks by winning 2–1 at Anfield in
1959, and he was in charge of the Potters in 1978 when
Blyth Spartans visited the Victoria Ground and, despite
being 2–1 down with a few minutes to go, the plucky
non-Leaguers bounced back to win 3–2.

BRIGHT SPARKS

The Brightwell brothers Ian and David both played for
Manchester City with some distinction but they arrived
at the Victoria Ground at the wrong end of their careers.
David arrived during the 1995/96 campaign on loan
from the Blues and played just once before returning
to Maine Road. Ian was signed from Walsall on a free

transfer and played four times during the 2001/02 season before his career really nose-dived with a move to Port Vale. The lads are the sons of Olympic athletes Ann Packer and Robbie Brightwell.

BERRY GAUDY?

George Berry was the first City player to sport an afro that accounted for roughly one-third of his total height. Of Caribbean descent, cult figure Berry was born in Germany, raised in the Midlands and played for Wales during a career in which he spent eight years at the Victoria Ground. After a 1987 3–1 home defeat to Manchester City, Berry, who based his hairstyle on the Jackson Five, endeared himself to Stokies by claiming in an after-match interview that the result 'Did me head in.' He played for the club between 1982 and 1990 before moving on to Peterborough United.

BERRY GOOD QUOTES

'My hair is now back to the bone. When I became follicly challenged in my mid-thirties I went through anger, denial and finally acceptance. It's a shame I'm not still playing or I could have got Gillette to sponsor my haircut.'

GB rues the fact that he can't join in with the recent re-emergence of afros

'I always thought Stoke should be back in the Premier League, along with another of my old clubs, Wolves. This season, I don't think they will finish massively higher than fourth from bottom, but I'd be happy with that.'

GB – happy to be proved wrong!

'Mind you, he can throw it further than I could kick it.'

GB on Rory Delap

'They wouldn't bother if I was playing badly. If I could get them to call me 'n****r' I knew I was doing my job. I wasn't upset by a few NF fans. I was upset if we lost 3–1.'

GB on the only way to respond to racists

ROONEY! ROONEY! ROONEY!

The Potters' youngest scorer of a hat-trick is Adam Rooney, who collected the matchball after a 5–1 away win at Brighton on 30 April 2006. Rooney was aged 18 years and 9 days at the time.

WORLD CUP POTTERS

The first two Potters to represent their country at the World Cup finals were Gordon Banks in 1970 when he kept goal for England in Mexico, and Sammy McIlroy who represented Northern Ireland in 1982.

PUT IT IN NEUTRAL!

City have played on neutral venues, including Wembley Stadium and the Millennium Stadium, on 23 occasions. Impressively, City have won four of their five appearances at Wembley – an 80 per cent success rate most teams would be happy to swap. The first occasion was in 1899 when the Potters reached the semi-final of the FA Cup where they faced Derby County at Molineux. The Rams triumphed 3–1 on the day to progress to the final. City have met Arsenal four times on neutral venues, in two FA Cup semi-finals and their subsequent replays, while the most unusual reason for playing on somebody else's patch was the FA Cup third place play-off in 1971 (don't ask!) when Everton's 3–2 win meant they could, after all, hire that open-top bus.

Here is the complete list:

FA Cup

Season/Versus	Score	Reason	Ground
1898/99 v Derby Co	1–3	S-F	Molineux
1906/07 v West Brom	0–2	R1 r	Villa Park
1907/08 v Gainsboro'	3–1	R2 r	City Ground
1909/10 v Exeter City	2–1	5RQ r	Craven Cottage
1926/27 v Rhyl	1–2	R1 r	Old Trafford
1930/31 v Man Utd	2–4	R3 2nd r	Anfield
1931/32 v Sunderland	2–1	R4 2nd r	Maine Road
1954/55 v Bury	3–3	R3 2nd r	Goodison Park
1954/55 v Bury	2–2	R3 3rd r	Anfield
1954/55 v Bury	3–2	R3 4th r	Old Trafford
1957/58 v Aston Villa	2–0	R3 2nd r	Molineux
1960/61 v Aldershot	3–0	R4 2nd r	Molineux
1970/71 v Huddersf'd T	1–0	R4 2nd r	Old Trafford
1970/71 v Arsenal	2–2	S-F	Hillsborough
1970/71 v Arsenal	0–2	S-F	Villa Park
1971/72 v Arsenal	1–1	S-F	Villa Park
1971/72 v Arsenal	1–2	S-F	Goodison Park
1971/72 v Everton	2–3	3/4 p/o	Selhurst Park
2010/11 v Bolton	5–0	S-F	Wembley
2010/11 v Man City	0–1	F	Wembley

League Cup

1963/64 v Scunth'pe Utd	1–0	R2 2nd r	Hillsborough
1971/72 v West Ham	0–0	S-F	Hillsborough
1971/72 v West Ham	3–2	S-F r	Old Trafford

Season/Versus	Score	Reason	Ground
1971/72 v Chelsea	2–1	Final	Wembley

League play-offs

2001/02 v Brentford	2–0	p/o Final	Millennium Stadium

Football League Trophy

1991/92 v Stockport Co	1–0	Final	Wembley
1999/2000 v Bristol C	2–1	Final	Wembley

Total record for neutral venues:
Pld 27   W 14   D 5   L 8   F 47   A 36

POTTERS v GALÁCTICOS

Tony Pulis's Austrian training camp has become almost legendary over the years and has helped strike up an unlikely friendship with Real Madrid who also use the same weeks and base as the Potters. In 2007, City and Madrid met in Irdning for a pre-season friendly that had originally been arranged with previous Galácticos boss Fabio Capello. Goals from Raul and Soldado gave Bernd Schuster's side a 2–0 win, but this wasn't the first meeting between the two clubs. In 1963, Madrid were the honoured guests for City's Centenary match on 24 April and a crowd believed to be in the region of 52,000 witnessed a 2–2 draw at the Victoria Ground.

PULIS SAID IT…

'If we treat the last 12 games any differently than we have the first 34, we will end up with our pants pulled down and our backsides slapped.'

In response to the question – can City survive?

'We are not at Crufts, we are at Battersea Dogs' Home. We go looking for strays, get them in and cuddle them.'

Matthew Etherington's £3 million purchase is explained

'The problem with foreign players is they go down and stay down. I was born in Wales, I played my football in England and we are different to them, I suppose. I am not having a go at him [Ballack], it is just their culture.'

On divers

'You can fool some of the people all of the time, and all of the people some of the time, but you cannot fool all of the people all of the time.'

Abraham Pulis on Arsène Wenger's damning verdict on City's tactics

'Arsène sent me a lovely letter and a signed Arsenal shirt. That was a really nice gesture and I appreciated it. What was said by Arsène Wenger is over, water under the bridge. He is a top-class manager with a top club and top players. We are competitive, sometimes you mis-time tackles. But we haven't got dirty players.'

Pulis and the professor kiss and make up

'We've shut Beattie down for this week.'

The City boss admits that James Beattie is, in fact, a robot

'I do not profess to be the person who will go onto the pitch and sing songs after the game – Brownie has got a good voice, I haven't. Brownie has got a full mop of hair, I haven't.'

Tony Pulis on what distinguishes him and Phil Brown, though there was no mention of the Cuprinol-style perma-tan Brown has applied annually

'If we win at Fulham, I will float around the marathon course.'

Pulis was forced to run the London Marathon like everyone else following City's 1–0 defeat

SARDINE ANYONE?

The 1934 FA Cup tie between Manchester City and the Potters still holds the record for the biggest crowd in a competitive English match, excluding, of course, games played at Wembley Stadium.

Some 84,569 people crammed into Maine Road that day to see Eric Brook's solitary goal send Manchester City through to the next round while at least etching Stoke's name into history.

THEY SAID IT ABOUT STANLEY MATTHEWS ...

'You're 32 – do you think you can make it for another couple of years?'

Blackpool manager Joe Smith in 1947 – Matthews would play on for almost another two decades!

'The man who taught us the way football should be played.'

Pelé lavishes praise on City's greatest player

'I grew up in an era when he was a god to those of us who aspired to play the game. He was a true gentleman and we shall never see his like again.'

Brian Clough – another legend the like of which we shall never see again

'It is not just in England where his name is famous. All over the world he is regarded as a true football genius.'

German legend Berti Vogts

'For me this man probably had the greatest name of any player ever, certainly in Britain. I don't think anyone since had a name so synonymous with football in England.'

Gordon Banks

BOOKED

Here are several books on City worth seeking out which have been published over the years:

Stoke City on This Day: History, Facts and Figures from Every Day of the Year, by Richard Murphy (2009)

. . . And She Laughed No More: Stoke City's Premiership Adventure, by Stephen Foster (2008)

Match of My Life – Stoke City: Sixteen Stars Relive Their Greatest Games, by Simon Lowe (2007)

The Legends of Stoke City, by Tony Matthews (2008)

Stoke City's Greatest Games, by Simon Lowe (2009)

She Stood There Laughing: A Man, His Son and Their Football Club, by Stephen Foster (2004)

Potters at War: Stoke City 1939–47, by Simon Lowe (2004)

Who's Who of Stoke City, by Tony Matthews (2008)

Tie Me to the Mast: The Football Season Has Begun, by David Johnson (2008)

You Could'ner make it up! The 25 Post-Waddington Stoke City Managers that Led to the Premier League! by D. Lee (2008)

Determined to Win, by George Eastham (1966)

The Science of Football – How to Play and Win, by George Eastham (1964)

My Life in Football, by Alan A'Court

The Working Man's Ballet, by Alan Hudson

Blue Blood, by Mike Doyle (2003)

The Waddington Years, by Alan Hudson (2008)

WORST KIT?

Fashion-wise, the 1990s were almost on a par with the 1980s with clothing disasters aplenty, so it's hardly surprising to learn that wearing the 1992/93 City away kit was almost an arrestable offence. Allegedly inspired by television interference, this is one kit that should have never have left the drawing board with its garish purple design and hideous jagged goal line across the upper chest. Just a nightmare from start to finish. . . .

(UN)LUCKY BREAK

There are no records that show how many black cats former City stalwart Denis Smith ran over during his time with the club, but he had the misfortune of having sustained the follwing: five broken legs, four broken noses, a cracked ankle, a broken collar bone, a chipped spine, most of his fingers and toes broken, as well as over 100 stitches at various times in Stoke colours – ouch!

WONG NUMBER

On 3 February 1945 Frank Wong Soo became the first player of Chinese extraction to play for England (and having checked through numerous volumes of stats – he still is the only one!). Indeed, Frank was the first non-white player of any ethnic background to represent England, long before Viv Anderson, the first 'official' black player, made his debut for England in 1979.

Frank was born in Buxton, Derbyshire, in 1914 and was the son of a Chinese father and an English mother. While rumours abounded that he did a nice dish of fried rice for dinner guests, he was one of the best inside forwards of the immediate pre-war era, certainly during his time at City, where he formed part of a legendary team that included players such as Sir Stanley Matthews and Neil Franklin. This famous trio played together in the England team that faced Scotland at Villa Park in 1945.

RORY DELAP: DID YOU KNOW?

- He was born on 6 July 1976 in Sutton Coldfield

- Rory is a former schoolboy javelin champion

- Martin O'Neill described Rory's throws as the equivalent of 'a corner or a free kick'

- His gargantuan throws average around 35 metres

- Wigan's Mario Melchiot described Delap as possessing 'one hell of a throw-in' and added he thought it was a 'great weapon'

- Delap doesn't do any extra strength exercises on his upper body and uses the main thrust of power from his shoulders and lower back muscles

- For the ball to reach his target faster, Delap throws it on a flat trajectory, releasing in such a way to cause large amounts of backspin. This helps to counter gravity so the ball will travel on a more level elevation, even though it is released at such a low angle – the ball literally darts in

- In the 2008/09 Premier League season Delap's throw-ins led directly to both goals scored in at least two matches. Both Stoke goals in the 3–2 loss to Everton on 14 September 2008 came about as a result of Delap's throw. Afterwards Everton manager David Moyes referred to Delap as the 'Human Sling'

- Rory Delap was selected for the Republic of Ireland national team in 1998 and has won eleven caps for the team

- Rory signed a deal for Southampton in 2001 for £4m, and represented the club in 132 matches, netting five goals. His bicycle kick in the match against Tottenham Hotspur won him the club's Goal of the Season award

- His throw-in v Arsenal in November 2008 was later measured at 45 metres – the world record is 46 metres!

- He was voted the Sir Stanley Matthews Potteries Footballer of the Year for 2008/09

QUOTES ON RORY

'I think he puts the ball better with his hands than his foot, it's fantastic. I have never seen anything like this in my life; 10 metres outside midfield, this boy puts the ball inside the area. Maybe it's not beautiful football, but it's effective.'

Luiz Felipe Scolari

'I have never seen anyone with a throw-in like Delap's and I believe his missiles have created 7 out of Stoke's 13 league goals this season. I had a long throw and used to practice them, but I could only just about get it in the box. My team-mate Perry Groves could throw it a long way and we have seen the likes of Dave Challinor and Andy Legg do it – but nothing like Delap. Most long throws tend to be a bit loopy, whereas Delap's are fired in like a free-kick – but even more dangerous.'

Lee Dixon

'It causes so many problems among the opposition defence. I think it's because they're so flat. They're not lofted into the air, he throws it pretty flat and it's very difficult for defenders to pick up the flight.'

Tony Pulis

KIT HISTORY

City haven't always played in red and white stripes – just ask your grandfather; he may be old enough to recall the days when the Potters played in some garish and unusual strips.

Stoke Ramblers wore red and blue hoops, white shorts and red and blue hooped socks, whereas plain old Stoke wore black and blue hoops, white shorts and black and blue socks up until 1883. From 1883 to 1891 the club wore the first strip that would be recognisable to modern-day fans, when they plumped for red and white stripes, white shorts and black socks, though they had various mixes of colours, including maroon shirts, white and blue shirts and white shirts and blue shorts.

Finally, in 1908, sense prevailed with the red and white stripes, white shorts and white socks being fairly consistent until 1983 when an abomination of a strip was thrust upon the Stokies for two years – with red sleeves, white chest and red pinstripes and red shorts and socks – it just wasn't City and from 1985 onwards tradition has won the day.

The stripes may have become fewer over the years, but at least it's clear that Stoke City FC have their own identity – long may that continue.

TJ!

TJ is the man who, more often than not, gets 'Delilah' ringing around grounds in England. A well-known figure among Potters fans, he is often enticed to begin the song by a chorus of 'Teeeeee Jaaaayyyyy!' and then, from out of a sea of red and white, one TJ would emerge, climb whatever he needed to climb and then hush the masses. When he has everyone's attention, he begins.

'At break of day when that man drove away I was waiting . . .' he shouts for all his worth and the City fans respond accordingly – in harmony, of course. TJ then continues: 'I crossed the street to her house and she opened the door . . .' and before you know it, 'Delilah' is in full swing. Nobody gets 'Delilah' going like TJ, whether at the Britannia Stadium or any other ground Stoke visit around the country. Look out for him in the North Stand on matchdays and, if necessary, buy that man a pint!

YANKEE DOODLE POTTERS

In January 2008 the Austin Aztex, who joined the United Soccer Leagues in 2009, and Stoke City announced a team partnership. The clubs will share training information and players, with Austin acting as a potential player resource for City in future years. The Potters hope the relationship will unearth untapped American talents, with Texas considered to be one of the hotbeds for US football talent. Stoke City also look to build an American fanbase by sending young players to get playing time and selling Stoke City merchandise in Austin. It sounds crazy but it might just work. . . .

MORE STATESIDE STOKIES

The Cleveland Stokers were a soccer team based in Cleveland, Ohio, which played in the United Soccer Association during 1967 and the North American Soccer League in 1968. Their home ground was Cleveland Stadium. Uniquely, the United league was made up of teams imported from foreign leagues and the 1967 Cleveland squad was actually the Stoke City first-team squad who had somehow got themselves mixed up in this odd experiment. New signing Gordon Banks, who had only just joined from Leicester City, was among the Potters squad that took part and the Stokers finished in second position in the Eastern Division. Following the 1967 season, the USA merged with the National Professional Soccer League to form the North American Soccer League with the teams from the former USA having to create their teams from scratch, thus ending City's involvement.

Peter Dobing top-scored with 7 goals in 8 games, while John Mahoney and Eric Skeels played 12 times; George Eastham played in 11 matches as did Alan Bloor. The full squad was: Gordon Banks, John Farmer, George Eastham, Eric Skeels, Peter Dobing, Maurice Setters, Bill Bentley, John Moore, Tony Allen, Harry Burrows, Alan Bloor, Roy Vernon, John Marsh, Mike Bernard, Terry Conroy and Paul Shardlow.

There is one link to the Potters which is worth mentioning and it happened a year after City officially pulled their players out of Cleveland. On 10 July 1968, at Cleveland Municipal Stadium, the Stokers hosted and defeated perhaps the greatest club team in the world when they beat Santos of Brazil 2–1 – a side that included Pelé, no less. City keeper Paul Shardlow, on loan for the summer, saved a penalty kick to preserve his team's lead and they held on for a famous victory. He had played

32 times for the Stokers that summer but, tragically, not long after returning to City, Shardlow collapsed and died of a heart attack during training on 14 October 1968 aged just 25.

HIP OR MISS MASCOT?

Stoke have two club mascots called Pottermus, and Pottermiss (a female version of Pottermus, of course). Pottermus was created when Stoke City moved to the Britannia Stadium in the 1997/98 season, while Pottermiss was created in the 2002/03 season for equality reasons.

Pottermus is bad to the bone and has been known to ride a motorcycle around the pitch in a leather jacket and he was the first club mascot to hold a motorcycle licence – not usually a prerequisite for the club furball.

He has also won the mascots' grand national on two occasions, further enhancing his cult status among the Potters' fans. He famously removed the head of Nuneaton Borough's mascot, a bear, much to the horror of the younger fans in the crowd, and also likes to use his wrestling skills on any visiting mascots though rumours he's the head of the notorious City hooligan outfit the Naughty Forty remain, at present, unproven.

DERBY DAY

City's traditional rivals are also geographically the closest – Port Vale. Though the rivalry runs deep and is as passionate as any in England, in recent years this has subsided somewhat due to City's progression up the football league ladder and Vale's descent into the bottom tier of the Football League. The first meeting was in October 1887 during an FA Cup tie but it would be another 33 years before the teams met again competitively. Being the second team in Stoke, the Valiants have spent most of their time in the shadow of their (ah-hem!) more successful neighbours, though the derby matches are always incredibly tight with no more than three goals scored in the past 15 meetings. Vale have lost just 2 of the last 13 games

Tony Pulis's close friend Micky Adams became manager at Vale in 2009 and it has been stated that relations between the two clubs will be friendlier for the foreseeable future – at least while both men are in charge. City may even send some players to Vale on loan to gain first-team experience – whether the fans will feel any differently is another matter entirely. The complete record of meetings between the clubs is:

2001/02
21 October   Port Vale 1–1 Stoke
League Division Two

10 February   Stoke 0–1 Port Vale
League Division Two

2000/01
17 September   Port Vale 1–1 Stoke
League Division Two

17 February   Stoke 1–1 Port Vale
League Division Two

5 March   Port Vale 2–1 Stoke
(Associate Members Cup)

1997/98
12 October   Stoke 2–1 Port Vale
League Division One

1 March   Port Vale 0–0 Stoke
League Division One

1996/97
13 October   Port Vale 1–1 Stoke
League Division One

20 April   Stoke 2–0 Port Vale
League Division One

1995/96
27 August   Stoke 0–1 Port Vale
League Division One

12 March   Port Vale 1–0 Stoke
League Division One

1994/95
14 March   Port Vale 1–1 Stoke
League Division One

22 April   Stoke 0–1 Port Vale
League Division One

1992/93
24 October   Stoke 2–1 Port Vale
League Division Two

16 November   Stoke 0–0 Port Vale
FA Cup

24 November   Port Vale 3–1 Stoke
FA Cup

3 March   Stoke 0–1 Port Vale
(Associate Members' Cup)

31 March   Port Vale 0–2 Stoke
League Division Two

1989/90
23 September   Stoke 1–1 Port Vale
Second Division

3 February   Port Vale 0–0 Stoke
Second Division

1956/57
10 October   Stoke 3–1 Port Vale
Second Division

29 April   Port Vale 2–2 Stoke
Second Division

1955/56
8 October   Port Vale 1–0 Stoke
Second Division

31 March   Stoke 1–1 Port Vale
Second Division

1954/55
4 September   Stoke 0–0 Port Vale
Second Division

25 April   Port Vale 0–1 Stoke
Second Division

1950/51
6 January   Stoke 2–2 Port Vale
FA Cup

8 January   Port Vale 0–1 Stoke
FA Cup

1932/33
22 October   Stoke 1–0 Port Vale
Second Division

4 March   Port Vale 1–3 Stoke
Second Division

1931/32
26 September   Stoke 4–0 Port Vale
Second Division

6 February   Port Vale 3–0 Stoke
Second Division

1930/31
13 December   Stoke 1–0 Port Vale
Second Division

18 April   Port Vale 0–0 Stoke
Second Division

1928/29
15 September   Stoke 2–1 Port Vale
Second Division

26 January   Port Vale 1–2 Stoke
Second Division

1927/28
5 November   Stoke 0–2 Port Vale
Second Division

17 March   Port Vale 0–0 Stoke
Second Division

1925/26
31 August   Port Vale 3–0 Stoke
Second Division

7 September   Stoke 0–3 Port Vale
Second Division

1924/25
20 September   Stoke 0–1 Port Vale
Second Division

24 January   Port Vale 2–0 Stoke
Second Division

1923/24
6 October   Stoke 1–0 Port Vale
Second Division

13 October   Port Vale 2–4 Stoke
Second Division

1921/22
24 September   Stoke 0–0 Port Vale
Second Division

1 October   Port Vale 0–1 Stoke
Second Division

7 January   Port Vale 2–4 Stoke
FA Cup

1920/21
2 October   Stoke 0–1 Port Vale
Second Division

25 September   Port Vale 2–1 Stoke
Second Division

1919/20
6 March   Port Vale 0–3 Stoke
Second Division

13 March   Stoke 0–0 Port Vale
Second Division

1887/88
15 October   Stoke 1–0 Port Vale
FA Cup

City's total record versus Port Vale:
Pld 52   W 19   D 17   L 16   F 54   A 49

OTHER RIVALRIES

Crewe Alexandra
Another rivalry based around locality above all else,
and a club which has fallen down the leagues in recent
years.

   With the Railwaymen in League 2, the Potters are
now seen as a more viable option for young players that
have historically chosen Crewe over Stoke owing to the
former's renowned youth policy. More recently players
are being seen to favour City because of their overall
stature in football.

Wolves
Owing to the demise of their main geographical rivals,
City fans have deemed it necessary to place more
emphasis on the games against Wolves as the two clubs
play each other more frequently in the League. There
is a history of hooligan activity surrounding this game,
which adds to the often intense atmosphere when the
two teams meet.

Cardiff
Included in a list of Stoke rivals, not for many football-related reasons, but because of the historical relationship between the two sets of supporters that has meant they have had one or two off-field battles in their time.

THE MANCS ARE COMING!

For some reason or other, Manchester City seem to have brought more fans than most to Stoke over the years with several mini-invasions springing to mind. In 1981 more than 10,000 Blues travelled to the Potteries to witness Trevor Francis's debut, and they left with beaming smiles after a 3–1 victory. The next occasion the Mancs came to town saw that defeat avenged, but for anybody who witnessed the colourful scenes on Boxing Day 1989, it was a day that will live long in the memory. More than 12,000 Manchester City fans arrived at the Victoria Ground in fancy dress with every kind of inflatable under the sun, from thousands of bananas to blow-up dolls, a Frankenstein, ET, hammers and even a camp bed. It was a fantastic sight and even the Blues' players ran out each carrying a huge inflatable banana. The effect seemed positive with the visitors going in 1–0 up at the break, but the Potters roared back after half-time with Peter Beagrie causing mayhem and Chris Kamara kicking anything that moved as Stoke won 3–1 on the day. The Stoke fans, incidentally, invaded Maine Road with upwards of 2,000 Pink Panthers later that season – a much more original idea! The Manchester City fans again turned out in force of the final day of the 1997/98 campaign with perhaps 6,000 filling the away end at the Britannia. The Blues won 5–2, but both teams were relegated as other results went against them.

FANZINE

The Oatcake is City's premier – and only – fanzine and, for those who live outside the area, it takes its name from a local 'delicacy', the North Staffordshire oatcake. The fanzine is known for its cartoons featuring stereotypes both from within the city of Stoke-on-Trent and from the world of football and is humorous, cutting, well-written and informative.

Costing £1.50, It has been running for well over 20 years and is now Stoke City's sole fanzine, following the demise of the superbly titled *A View to a Kiln*. Edited by Martin Smith, for many City fans *The Oatcake* is a meatier option than the official matchday programme.

CITY FANS

Historically Stoke fans have something of a bad reputation having once been described as one of the main purveyors of football hooliganism in the mid-1990s – surely not? However, that perception has changed since the turn of the new century, as the Stoke faithful have, instead, become perhaps the most passionate supporters in the Premier League.

In a 2009 survey carried out by Sky TV, the fans at the Britannia Stadium were found to be the loudest in the league, after being recorded at 101.8 decibels and beating the likes of Liverpool and Newcastle supporters to the top spot – tell us something we didn't already know. Many people believe that the loyalty is due to the fact that City are deemed to be a somewhat unfashionable outfit and in typical Premier League snobbery, not one of the 'elite'. The team's football was heavily criticised during the 2008/09 campaign and this led to a 'them and us' mentality among City fans and the players alike – a kind of 'no-one likes us, we don't care' attitude. The aim, therefore, was to disappoint the club's numerous critics by creating a cauldron-like, intimidating atmosphere at the Britannia Stadium to unsettle the strutting, glove- and tights-wearing superstars who may have felt they were a cut above the City players. It worked a treat! More of the same, please!

CELEBRITY CITY FANS

Famous City supporters include the likes of broadcaster and former *They Think It's All Over* presenter Nick Hancock (see separate entry) and former England cricket all-rounder Dominic Cork. Both men are known to attend matches as regularly as possible. Cork, however, once played for Derby County in a celebrity indoor football tournament owing to the lack of a Stoke team entering the competition. Darts player Adrian Lewis and *Midsomer Murders* writer Jeremy Paul are also City fans.

IS THIS REALLY HOW 'DELILAH' BEGAN?

Allegedly, an upper-class woman wandered past a group of City fans, who were parked outside a pub, amid the predictable and Neanderthal cries of 'Get yer knockers out for the lads.' (Original, lads!) Upon hearing this, a policeman wandered over and asked the City fans to sing something more appropriate at which point some guy (now a legend) started singing the Tom Jones classic 'Delilah'. Others joined in, they repeated it at the match, and the rest is history!

Another explanation could be because of a fan in the 1970s blessed with the same name as Tom Jones. Rather than quote Henry Fielding (author of the the classic book

Tom Jones) at him, fellow fans started singing 'Delilah' at the Victoria Ground in tribute. There's probably a million other explanations and one of them is likely to be the truth – unless, of course, you know better?

The song often garners a reaction of some kind from opposing fans, and during a match against Manchester City in the 1980s, a delay owing to a fire alarm meant Maine Road was largely silent as the crowd awaited the players' entrance. A rousing chorus of 'Delilah' struck up and, when the 2,500 Potters fans finished, the Man City fans broke out in applause.

HANCOCK'S HALF OURS

City's most famous fan and loyal supporter is undoubtedly comedian and television presenter Nick Hancock. A boyhood Potter, he rarely misses the opportunity to tell the nation he is a long-suffering City fan.

In September 2001, he paid £20,000 at Sotheby's Football Memorabilia auction in London for the FA Cup winners' medal awarded to Sir Stanley Matthews in 1953. The same year, he successfully bid for Gordon Banks' blue World Cup 1970 international cap for £8,225 at auction. For all that, we'll forgive him for the Morrisons advert!

Here are a couple of his classic quotes:

'My earliest memory is of the 1969/70 season, then the next two years were really big ones for Stoke. I just presumed the rest of my life would be FA Cup semi-finals, League Cup finals and 2–1 home victories.'

'My grandfather would always lose the car after parking up for a home game. It got to the stage where we would head straight to the police station after a match and they'd be waiting there to tell us where we'd parked.'

LADIES FIRST ...

Stoke City Ladies were formed in 2001 and enjoyed a terrific first season, finishing third in the West Midlands League Division One and in turn winning a place in the Premier Division after successfully negotiating the play-offs. In 2008/09 they finally gained promotion to the West Midlands Combination League. The ladies play their home fixtures at the Motiva Stadium on Yarnfield Lane

FIRST IN, FIRST OUT

The Potters became a professional football club in 1885 and three years later they were one of only 12 clubs who formed the 'English Football League'. Stoke played their first ever Football League game against West Bromwich Albion on 8 September 1888 in front of a crowd of around 4,500. The fledgling club's first victory was a fortnight later when they beat Notts County 3–0, but it was to be one of only four victories. Unfortunately, Stoke ended that first season in last place after failing to pick up at least a draw in their final fixture against Accrington Stanley.

1888/89: Stoke's first full season results:

West Bromwich Albion	home	0–2
Aston Villa	away	1–5
Notts County	home	3–0

Accrington	home	2–4
Preston North End	away	0–7
Bolton Wanderers	away	1–2
Burnley	home	4–3
Blackburn Rovers	away	2–5
Aston Villa	home	1–1
Preston North End	home	0–3
Wolverhampton Wanderers	home	0–1
Notts County	away	3–0
Blackburn Rovers	home	2–1
Burnley	away	1–2
Everton	home	0–0
Wolverhampton Wanderers	away	1–4
West Bromwich Albion	away	0–2
Everton	away	1–2
Bolton Wanderers	home	2–2
Derby County	away	1–2
Derby County	home	1–1
Accrington	away	0–2

The final table 1888/89

	P		HOME					AWAY				Pts
		W	D	L	F	A	W	D	L	F	A	
1 Preston	22	10	1	0	39	7	8	3	0	35	8	40
2 Aston Villa	22	10	0	1	44	16	2	5	4	17	27	29
3 Wolves	22	8	2	1	31	14	4	2	5	20	23	28
4 Blackburn	22	7	4	0	44	22	3	2	6	22	23	26
5 Bolton	22	6	0	5	35	30	4	2	5	28	29	22
6 West Brom	22	6	2	3	25	24	4	0	7	15	22	22
7 Accrington	22	5	3	3	26	17	1	5	5	22	31	20
8 Everton	22	8	0	3	24	17	1	2	8	11	30	20
9 Burnley	22	6	3	2	21	19	1	0	10	21	43	17
10 Derby Co	22	5	1	5	22	20	2	1	8	19	41	16
11 Notts Co	22	4	2	5	25	32	1	0	10	15	41	12
12 Stoke City	22	3	4	4	15	18	1	0	10	11	33	12

YOU'RE GONNA WIN FOUR ALL!

OK, a slight amend on the terrace chant, but it leads us nicely into City's highest-scoring home draws. The Potters have shared eight goals on three occasions, drawing 4–4 with Burnley in November 1963 and then repeating the scoreline a fortnight later against Sheffield Wednesday – typical; you wait almost 100 years for one and then two come along at once. To confirm the rarity of this scoreline, it would be another 19 years before City drew 4–4 again, this time with Luton Town in 1982 – and there's been no more since!

Away from home there have also been three 4–4 draws. The first was at Bolton Wanderers in 1892, the next was against Charlton Athletic at The Valley in 1929 and the last 4–4 result on the road was at Ninian Park against Cardiff City in 1959. There have been no eight-goal thrillers in cup competitions though there have been nine 3–3 draws to date.

PULIS SAID WHAT?

'I am not too concerned about how much I like them or how well I know them. I had never really met Dave Kemp before, but I felt he was right for me when I went to Portsmouth. I have to really work with someone like that who I feel will be strong enough to say if he thinks things are not going well. I don't really like working with people who just agree all the time.'

Saying no to yes men! (July 2009)

'We won't get carried away because we know we have to bring in players if we are to push on. You are criticised by supporters for not bringing in players; I could bring in a busload of players, but if they are no good the first to moan are people in the seats. So you have to bring in good players within the budget you are working to.'

Bemoaning lack of funds to strengthen his squad (August 2007)

'It's fantastic to be recognised by the community. This honour is very special. I wish my primary school teachers could be here to see me receiving the award as I think they would be very proud.'

On accepting an honorary degree from Staffordshire University (July 2009)

THE BEAST

Man-mountain Jon Parkin joined City permanently from Hull City in 2007 having spent six games on loan at the Britannia the season before. The 6ft 4in striker scored three goals in his six-game loan spell and was a popular figure among the City fans. Looking more like a darts player than a footballer, Parkin had quick feet for a big man and Tony Pulis paid £275,000 to bring the man nicknamed 'The Beast' to the Potters. He enjoyed playing his part in helping the club to the Premier League for the first time, though he only scored two goals in 29 Championship matches. He was injured during a freak golfing accident before the 2007/08 campaign and explained, 'I was driving a golf cart, but didn't realise how steep the hill was. One thing led to another and it ended up on its roof. Steve Simonsen was with me and he was a bit dazed. I grazed my leg, which has taken time to heal. But I am now banned from driving them again.'

The song 'Feed the Beast and he will score' caught on before he moved to Preston North End in August 2008.

PLAYER OF THE SEASON

Here is a list of City legends that were voted the club's Player of the Year. The first official club award was handed out at the end of the 1977/78 campaign with Howard Kendall being the first recipient. Peter Fox has won the award three times and the only other person to win it more than once is Mickey Thomas, who first won it in 1983 and then again in 1991.

The complete list is:

1977/78	Howard Kendall
1978/79	Mike Doyle
1979/80	Alan Dodd
1980/81	Peter Fox
1981/82	Peter Fox
1982/83	Mickey Thomas
1983/84	Steve Bould
1984/85	Sammy McIlroy
1985/86	Keith Bertschin
1986/87	Lee Dixon
1987/88	Steve Parkin
1988/89	Chris Kamara
1989/90	Peter Fox
1990/91	Mickey Thomas
1991/92	Wayne Biggins
1992/93	Mark Stein
1993/94	Ian Cranson
1994/95	Larus Sigurdsson
1995/96	Ray Wallace and Mark Prudhoe
1996/97	Andy Griffin
1997/98	Justin Whittle
1998/99	Kevin Keen
1999/2000	James O'Connor
2000/01	Brynjar Gunnarsson
2001/02	Wayne Thomas

2002/03	Sergei Shtaniuk
2003/04	Ade Akinbiyi
2004/05	Clint Hill
2005/06	Carl Hoefkens
2006/07	Danny Higginbotham
2007/08	Liam Lawrence
2008/09	Abdoulaye Faye
2009/10	Matthew Etherington
2010/11	Robert Huth
2011/12	Peter Crouch

STATUESQUE TRIBUTES

Statues of two of City's greatest players were unveiled in 2001 and 2008. The first was for Sir Stanley Matthews and the second was for legendary Stoke and England keeper Gordon Banks. On 12 July 2008, Pelé and Archbishop Desmond Tutu travelled to the Britannia Stadium for the ceremony to celebrate Banks' career with the unveiling of a bronze statue in his honour.

There was also a celebrity football match featuring a Banks XI and a Pelé XI – the Brazil legend saw his side triumph 5–1. Pelé is no stranger to Stoke having scored twice during a 3–2 win at the Victoria Ground in 1969 for his Brazilian club side Santos – a year later Banks and Pelé would provide one of the most memorable moments in the history of the World Cup when Banks somehow managed to keep out Pelé's bullet header during England's clash with Brazil at the 1970 finals.

'I score more than 1,000 goals in my life, but the goal I don't score they remember!' said Pelé. 'Gordon and I became close friends in the United States.'

The statue was created by local artist Andrew Edwards and was the brainchild of Irish author Don Mullen who has written a book about Banks entitled *The Hero Who Could Fly*.

YOUNG PLAYER OF THE SEASON

As voted for by fellow team-mates, the Young Player of the Season award was launched in 2003 and the list of winners thus far is:

2003/04	Darel Russell
2004/05	John Halls
2005/06	Paul Gallagher
2006/07	Carl Dickinson and Martin Paterson
2007/08	Ryan Shawcross
2008/09	Ryan Shawcross
2009/10	Ryan Shawcross
2010/11	Asmir Begovic
2011/12	Ryan Shotton

ACCRINGTON STANLEY – WHO ARE THEY?

City have only met the team named after one half of Laurel and Hardy on two occasions. During the 1926/27 Division Three (North) campaign, the Potters won 1–0 in Lancashire and repeated the score at the Victoria Ground four months later. Since then the teams have avoided each other in the League hence most City fans knowing little or nothing about the Accies.

THE BEST OF THE BEST: APPEARANCE RECORDS

Here are a list of City's 'mosts' and 'firsts' – legends to a man!

Most Appearances (League & Cup)
Eric Skeels – 606 (1960–76)

Most Appearances (League)
Eric Skeels – 507 (1960–76)

Most Appearances (including wartime)
John McCue – 675 (1940–60)

Most Consecutive Appearances
Tony Allen – 148 (1960–3)

First Player to Reach 100 League Appearances
Alf Underwood in 1892/93 season

First Player to Reach 200 League Appearances
Tommy Clare in 1896/97 season

First Player to Reach 300 League Appearances
Bob McGrory in 1931/32 season

First Player to Reach 400 League Appearances
John McCue in 1959/60 season

First Player to Reach 500 League Appearances
Eric Skeels in 1974/75 season

Appearances Top Ten (including wartime)

John McCue	675
Frank Mountford	608
Eric Skeels	606
Frank Bowyer	598
Bob McGrory	511
Denis Smith	493
Alan Bloor	484
Tommy Sale	483
Peter Fox	477
Tony Allen	473

THE BEST OF THE BEST: GOALSCORING RECORDS

Leading Goalscorer (League & Cup)
John Ritchie – 171 (1963–6 & 1969–74)

Leading Goalscorer (League)
Freddie Steele – 140 (1934–49)

Leading Goalscorer (including wartime)
Tommy Sale – 282 (1930–6 & 1938–47)

Most Goals in a Season
Charlie Wilson – 38 (Division Two & FA Cup 1927/28)

Most League goals in a season
Freddie Steele – 33 (Division One 1936/37)

Most goals in a game
Neville Coleman – 7 (versus Lincoln City 23 February
   1957)

THE BEST OF THE BEST: INTERNATIONAL RECORDS

First player to be capped
Edward Johnson (England) v Wales (15 March 1880)

First Scotsman to be capped
Tommy Hyslop v England – 1896

First Welshmen to be capped
Mart Watkins, Dr Leigh Richmood Roose & Sammy
   Meredith v England – 1902

First Irishman to be capped
Jack Sheridan v England – 1905

Most Capped Player
Gordon Banks (England) 37

SCFC PLAYERS' PLAYER OF THE YEAR AWARD

In 2003 a new award was introduced by the Potters – the Stoke City Players' Player of the Year Award, a chance for team-mates to show their appreciation. The award has matched the Supporters' Player of the Season award three times out of six.
The winners:

2003/04	Wayne Thomas
2004/05	Steve Simonsen
2005/06	Steve Simonsen
2006/07	Danny Higginbotham
2007/08	Liam Lawrence
2008/09	Abdoulaye Faye
2009/10	Matthew Etherington
2010/11	Robert Huth
2011/12	Robert Huth/Ryan Shawcross

YOUNGEST/OLDEST

Peter Bullock, aged 16 years and 163 days, remains the youngest player to represent City to date. The teenager made his debut during a 4–1 defeat away to Swansea on 19 April 1958, scoring the Potters' only goal. Stanley Matthews' record for being the oldest player to play for Stoke is unlikely to be beaten – he was 50 years and 5 days old when he pulled on the red and white jersey for the last time during a 3–1 win over Fulham in April 1958.

TRANSFER RECORDS

The £10m City paid Tottenham for Peter Crouch in 2011 is the club's record transfer fee paid. Previously it was the £5.5m paid to Reading for the services of striker Dave Kitson in July 2008. Exactly a year later, City paid £3m for the services of Dean Whitehead and the fee could eventually rise to £5m. The record fee received was more than a decade old, with QPR's £2.75m purchase of Mike Sheron in July 1997 holding firm for 12 years, until Seyi Olofinjana joined Hull City in July 2009 for £3m. However, in January 2011 Wolfsburg paid £4.5 for Tuncay – the current club record for a received fee.

ACADEMY PLAYER OF THE SEASON

A prestigious honour for the club's emerging talent, here is a list of winners since the introduction of the award in 1994:

1994/95	Mark Birch
1995/96	Dean Crowe
1996/97	Robert Heath
1997/98	James O'Connor
1998/99	Marc Goodfellow
1999/2000	Gareth Owen
2000/01	Andy Wilkinson
2001/02	Matt Armstrong
2002/03	Richard Keogh
2003/04	Jermaine Palmer
2004/05	Martin Paterson
2005/06	Ryan Shotton
2006/07	Tom Thorley
2007/08	Nathaniel Wedderburn
2008/09	Andrew Nicholls
2009/10	Louis Moult

KITS AND SPONSORS

Here are a list of shirt sponsors and kit suppliers from 1974 up until the present day:

Season	Kit Supplier	Sponsor
1974/75	Admiral	none
1975/76–1980/81	Umbro	none
1981/82–1984/85	Umbro	Ricoh
1985/86	Umbro	none
1986/87	Hi-Tec	Crystal Tiles
1987/88–1988/89	Admiral	Crystal Tiles
1989/90	Scoreline	Crystal Tiles
1990/91	Matchwinner	Fradley Homes
1991/92–1992/93	Matchwinner	Ansells
1993/94–1994/95	Asics	Carling
1995/96	Asics	Broxap
1996/97	Asics	Asics
1997/98–2000/01	Asics	Britannia
2000/01–2002/03	Le Coq Sportif	Britannia
2003/04–2006/07	Puma	Britannia
2007/08	Le Coq Sportif	Britannia
2008/09	Le Coq Sportif	Britannia
2009/10	Adidas	Britannia
2010/11	Adidas	Britannia
2011/12	Adidas	Britannia
2012/13	Adidas	Bet365

FA CUP COMPLETE HISTORY

Have you ever wanted to know who the Potters have come up against in the most famous club competition in the world? Well here it is with a season-by-season breakdown of who City played, where and what the outcome was:

1883/84
1st Round – Manchester (h) 1–2 (this was neither
    Manchester City or Manchester United who didn't
    exist at this point)

1884/85
1st Round – Queen's Park (Glasgow) (a) – walkover

1885/86
1st Round – Crewe Alexandra (h) 2–2
1st Round Replay – Crewe Alexandra (a) 0–1

1886/87
1st Round – Caernarfon Wanderers (h) 10–1
2nd Round – Crewe Alexandra (a) 4–6

1887/88
1st Round – Burslem Port Vale (h) 1–0
2nd Round – Over Wanderers (a) 2–0
3rd Round – Oswestry (h) 3–0
4th Round – bye
5th Round – West Bromwich Albion (a) 1–4

1889/90
1st Round – Old Westminsters (h) 3–0
2nd Round – Everton (h) 4–2
Quarter-Final – Wolverhampton Wanderers (a) 0–4
    (declared void)
Quarter-Final – Wolverhampton Wanderers (a) 0–8
    (unfortunately declared valid!)

1890/91
1st Round – Preston North End (h) 3–0
2nd Round – Aston Villa (h) 3–0
Quarter-Final – Notts County (h) 0–1

1891/92
1st Round – Casuals (h) 3–0 (replay ordered – don't ask!)
1st Round – Casuals (a) 3–0
2nd Round – Burnley (a) 3–1
Quarter-Final – Sunderland (h) 2–2
Quarter-Final Replay – Sunderland (a) 0–4

1892/93
1st Round – Accrington (a) 1–2

1893/94
1st Round – Everton (h) 1–0
2nd Round – Sheffield Wednesday (a) 0–1

1894/95
1st Round – Newton Heath (a) 3–2
2nd Round – Wolverhampton Wanderers (a) 0–2

1895/96
1st Round – Tottenham Hotspur (h) 5–0
2nd Round – Burnley (a) 1–1
2nd Round Replay – Burnley (h) 7–1
Quarter-Final – Wolverhampton Wanderers (a) 0–3

1896/97
1st Round – Glossop North End (h) 5–2
2nd Round – Preston North End (a) 1–2

1897/98
1st Round – Bury (a) 2–1
2nd Round – Everton (h) 0–0
2nd Round Replay – Everton (a) 1–5

1898/99
1st Round – Sheffield Wednesday (a) 2–2
1st Round Replay – Sheffield Wednesday (h) 2–0

2nd Round – Small Heath (h) 2–2
2nd Round Replay – Small Heath (a) 2–1
Quarter-Final – Tottenham Hotspur (h) 4–1
Semi-Final – Derby County (n) 1–3 (played at
   Molineux)

1899/1900
1st Round – Liverpool (h) 0–0
1st Round Replay – Liverpool (a) 0–1

1900/01
Q – Glossop (h) 1–0
1st Round – Small Heath (h) 1–1
1st Round Replay – Small Heath (a) 1–2

1901/02
1st Round – Aston Villa (h) 2–2
1st Round Replay – Aston Villa (a) 2–1
2nd Round – Bristol Rovers (a) 1–0
Quarter-Final – Nottingham Forest (a) 0–2

1902/03
1st Round – Glossop (a) 3–2
2nd Round – Nottingham Forest (a) 0–0
2nd Round Replay – Nottingham Forest (h) 2–0
Quarter–Final – Derby County (a) 0–3

1903/04
1st Round – Aston Villa (h) 2–3

1904/05
1st Round – Grimsby Town (h) 2–0
2nd Round – Everton (h) 0–4

1905/06
1st Round – Blackburn Rovers (h) 1–0
2nd Round – Birmingham City (h) 0–1

1906/07
1st Round – West Bromwich Albion (a) 1–1
1st Round Replay – West Bromwich Albion (h) 2–2
1st Round 2nd Replay – West Bromwich Albion (n) 0–2
  (at Villa Park)

1907/08
1st Round – Lincoln City (h) 5–0
2nd Round – Gainsborough Trinity (h) 1–1
2nd Round Replay – Gainsborough Trinity (a) 2–2
2nd Round 2nd Replay – Gainsborough Trinity (n) 3–1
  (at the City Ground, Nottingham)
3rd Round – Portsmouth (a) 1–0
Quarter-Final – Wolverhampton Wanderers (h) 0–1

1908/09
1st Round – Sheffield Wednesday (a) 0–5

1909/10
5th Qualifying Round – Exeter City (h) 0–0
5th Qualifying Round Replay – Exeter City (a) 1–1
5th Qualifying Round 2nd Replay – Exeter City (n) 2–1
  (at Craven Cottage)
1st Round – Newcastle United (h) 1–1
1st Round Replay – Newcastle United (a) 1–2

1910/11
5th Qualifying Round – Lincoln City (h) 4–0
1st Round – Manchester City (h) 1–2

1912/13
1st Round – Reading (h) 2–2
1st Round Replay – Reading (a) 0–3

1913/14
5th Qualifying Round – Barrow (h) 3–1
1st Round – Aston Villa (a) 0–4

1919/20
1st Round – Bury (a) 0–2

1920/21
1st Round – Wolverhampton Wanderers (a) 2–3

1921/22
1st Round – Port Vale (a) 4–2
2nd Round – Northampton Town (a) 2–2
2nd Round Replay – Northampton Town (h) 3–0
3rd Round – Aston Villa (h) 0–0
3rd Round Replay – Aston Villa (a) 0–4

1922/23
1st Round – Blyth Spartans (a) 3–0
2nd Round – Bury (a) 1–3

1923/24
1st Round – Leeds United (a) 0–1

1924/25
1st Round – Leicester City (a) 0–3

1925/26
3rd Round – Wigan Borough (a) 5–2
4th Round – Swansea Town (a) 3–6

1926/27
1st Round – Rhyl Athletic (a) 1–1
1st Round Replay – Rhyl Athletic (h) 1–1
1st Round 2nd Replay – Rhyl Athletic (n) 1–2 (at Old
   Trafford)

1927/28
3rd Round – Gillingham (h) 6–1
4th Round – Bolton Wanderers (h) 4–2

5th Round – Manchester City (a) 1–0
Quarter-Final – Arsenal (a) 1–4

1928/29
3rd Round – Arsenal (a) 1–2

1929/30
3rd Round – Doncaster Rovers (a) 0–1

1930/31
3rd Round – Manchester United (h) 3–3
3rd Round Replay – Manchester United (a) 0–0
3rd Round 2nd Replay – Manchester United (n) 2–4 (at Anfield)

1931/32
3rd Round – Hull City (h) 3–0
4th Round – Sunderland (a) 1–1
4th Round Replay – Sunderland (h) 1–1
4th Round 2nd Replay – Sunderland (n) 2–1 (at Maine Road)
5th Round – Bury (a) 0–3

1932/33
3rd Round – Southampton (h) 1–0
4th Round – Middlesbrough (a) 1–4

1933/34
3rd Round – Bradford Park Avenue (h) 3–0
4th Round – Blackpool (h) 3–0
5th Round – Chelsea (h) 3–1
Quarter-Final – Manchester City (a) 0–1

1934/35
3rd Round – Swansea Town (a) 1–4

1935/36
3rd Round – Millwall (a) 0–0
3rd Round Replay – Millwall (h) 4–0
4th Round – Manchester United (h) 0–0
4th Round Replay – Manchester United (a) 2–0
5th Round – Barnsley (a) 1–2

1936/37
3rd Round – Birmingham (h) 4–1
4th Round – Preston North End (a) 1–5

1937/38
3rd Round – Derby County (a) 2–1
4th Round – Bradford Park Avenue (a) 1–1
4th Round Replay – Bradford Park Avenue (h) 1–2

1938/39
3rd Round – Leicester City (h) 1–1
3rd Round Replay – Leicester City (a) 1–2

1945/46
3rd Round 1st Leg – Burnley (h) 3–1
3rd Round 2nd Leg – Burnley (a) 1–2 (won 4–3 on
    aggregate)
4th Round 1st Leg – Sheffield United (h) 2–0
4th Round 2nd Leg – Sheffield United (a) 2–3 (won 4–3
    on aggregate)
5th Round 1st Leg – Sheffield Wednesday (h) 2–0
5th Round 2nd Leg – Sheffield Wednesday (a) 0–0 (won
    2–0 on aggregate)
Quarter-Final 1st Leg – Bolton Wanderers (h) 0–2
Quarter-Final 2nd Leg – Bolton Wanderers (a) 0–0 (lost
    0–2 on aggregate)

1946/47
3rd Round – Tottenham Hotspur (a) 2–2
3rd Round Replay – Tottenham Hotspur (h) 1–0

4th Round – Chester (a) 0–0
4th Round Replay – Chester (h) 3–2
5th Round – Sheffield United (h) 0–1

1947/48
3rd Round – Mansfield Town (a) 4–2
4th Round – Queens Park Rangers (a) 0–3

1948/49
3rd Round – Swindon Town (a) 3–1
4th Round – Blackpool (h) 1–1
4th Round – Blackpool (a) 1–0
5th Round – Hull City (h) 0–2

1949/50
3rd Round – Tottenham Hotspur (h) 0–1

1950/51
3rd Round – Port Vale (h) 2–2
3rd Round Replay – Port Vale (a) 1–0
4th Round – West Ham United (h) 1–0
5th Round – Newcastle United (h) 2–4

1951/52
3rd Round – Sunderland (a) 0–0
3rd Round Replay – Sunderland (h) 3–1
4th Round – Swindon Town (a) 1–1
4th Round Replay – Swindon Town (h) 0–1

1952/53
3rd Round Replay – Wrexham (h) 2–1
4th Round – Halifax Town (a) 0–1

1953/54
3rd Round – Hartlepool United (h) 6–2
4th Round – Leicester City (h) 0–0
4th Round Replay – Leicester City (a) 1–3

1954/55

3rd Round – Bury (a) 1–1

3rd Round Replay – Bury (h) 1–1

3rd Round 2nd Replay – Bury (n) 3–3 (at Goodison Park)

3rd Round 3rd Replay – Bury (n) 2–2 (at Anfield)

3rd Round 4th Replay – Bury (n) 3–2 (at Old Trafford)

4th Round – Swansea Town (a) 1–3

1955/56

3rd Round – Exeter City (a) 0–0

3rd Round Replay – Exeter City (h) 3–0

4th Round – Leicester City (a) 3–3

4th Round Replay – Leicester City (h) 2–1

5th Round – Newcastle United (a) 1–2

1956/57

3rd Round – Arsenal (a) 2–4

1957/58

3rd Round – Aston Villa (h) 1–1

3rd Round Replay – Aston Villa (a) 3–3

3rd Round 2nd Replay – Aston Villa (n) 2–0 (at Molineux)

4th Round – Middlesbrough (h) 3–1

5th Round – Bolton Wanderers (a) 1–2

1958/59

3rd Round – Oldham Athletic (h) 5–1

4th Round – Ipswich Town (h) 0–1

1959/60

3rd Round – Preston North End (h) 1–1

3rd Round Replay – Preston North End (a) 1–3

1960/61
3rd Round – West Ham United (a) 2–2
3rd Round Replay – West Ham United (h) 1–0
4th Round – Aldershot (h) 0–0
4th Round Replay – Aldershot (a) 0–0
4th Round 2nd Replay – Aldershot (n) 3–0 (at Molineux)
5th Round – Newcastle United (a) 1–3

1961/62
3rd Round – Leicester City (a) 1–1
3rd Round Replay – Leicester City (h) 5–2
4th Round – Blackburn Rovers (h) 0–1

1962/63
3rd Round – Leeds United (a) 1–3

1963/64
3rd Round – Portsmouth (h) 4–1
4th Round – Ipswich Town (a) 1–1
4th Round Replay – Ipswich Town (h) 1–0
5th Round – Swansea Town (h) 2–2
5th Round Replay – Swansea Town (a) 0–2

1964/65
3rd Round – Blackpool (h) 4–1
4th Round – Manchester United (h) 0–0
4th Round Replay – Manchester United (a) 0–1

1965/66
3rd Round – Walsall (h) 0–2

1966/67
3rd Round – Manchester United (a) 0–2

1967/68
3rd Round – Cardiff City (h) 4–1
4th Round – West Ham United (h) 0–3

1968/69
3rd Round – York City (a) 2–0
4th Round – Halifax Town (h) 1–1
4th Round Replay – Halifax Town (a) 3–0
5th Round – Chelsea (a) 2–3

1969/70
3rd Round – Oxford United (a) 0–0
3rd Round – Oxford United (h) 3–2
4th Round – Watford (a) 0–1

1970/71
3rd Round – Millwall (h) 2–1
4th Round – Huddersfield Town (h) 3–3
4th Round Replay – Huddersfield Town (a) 0–0
4th Round 2nd Replay – Huddersfield Town (n) 1–0 (at Old Trafford)
5th Round – Ipswich Town (h) 0–0
5th Round Replay – Ipswich Town (a) 1–0
Quarter-Final – Hull City (a) 3–2
Semi-Final – Arsenal (n) 2–2 (at Hillsborough)
Semi-Final Replay – Arsenal (n) 0–2 (at Villa Park)

1971/72
3rd Round – Chesterfield (h) 2–1
4th Round – Tranmere Rovers (a) 2–2
4th Round Replay – Tranmere Rovers (h) 2–0
5th Round – Hull City (h) 4–1
Quarter-Final – Manchester United (a) 1–1
Quarter–Final Replay – Manchester United (h) 2–1
Semi-Final – Arsenal (n) 1–1 (at Villa Park)
Semi-Final Replay – Arsenal (n) 1–2 (at Goodison Park)

1972/73
3rd Round – Manchester City (a) 2–3

1973/74
3rd Round – Bolton Wanderers (a) 2–3

1974/75
3rd Round – Liverpool (a) 0–2

1975/76
3rd Round – Tottenham Hotspur (a) 1–1
3rd Round Replay – Tottenham Hotspur (h) 2–1
4th Round – Manchester City (h) 1–0
5th Round – Sunderland (h) 0–0
5th Round Replay – Sunderland (a) 1–2

1976/77
3rd Round – Everton (a) 0–2

1977/78
3rd Round – Tilbury (h) 4–0
4th Round – Blyth Spartans (h) 2–3

1978/79
3rd Round – Oldham Athletic (h) 0–1

1979/80
3rd Round – Burnley (a) 0–1

1980/81
3rd Round – Wolverhampton Wanderers (h) 2–2
3rd Round Replay – Wolverhampton Wanderers (a) 1–2

1981/82
3rd Round – Norwich City (h) 0–1

1982/83
3rd Round – Sheffield United (a) 0–0
3rd Round Replay – Sheffield United (h) 3–2
4th Round – Liverpool (a) 0–2

1983/84
3rd Round – Everton (h) 0–2

1984/85
3rd Round – Luton Town (a) 1–1
3rd Round Replay – Luton Town (h) 2–3

1985/86
3rd Round – Notts County (h) 0–2

1986/87
3rd Round – Grimsby Town (a) 1–1
3rd Round Replay – Grimsby Town (h) 1–1
3rd Round 2nd Replay – Grimsby Town (h) 6–0
4th Round – Cardiff City (h) 2–1
5th Round – Coventry City (h) 0–1

1987/88
3rd Round – Liverpool (h) 0–0
3rd Round Replay – Liverpool (a) 0–1

1988/89
3rd Round – Crystal Palace (h) 1–0
4th Round – Barnsley (h) 3–3
4th Round Replay – Barnsley (a) 1–2

1989/90
3rd Round – Arsenal (h) 0–1

1990/91
1st Round – Telford United (a) 0–0
1st Round Replay – Telford United (h) 1–0
2nd Round – Burnley (a) 0–2

1991/92
1st Round – Telford United (h) 0–0
1st Round Replay – Telford United (a) 1–2

1992/93
1st Round – Port Vale (h) 0–0
1st Round Replay – Port Vale (a) 1–3

1993/94
3rd Round – Bath City (h) 0–0
3rd Round Replay – Bath City (a) 4–1
4th Round – Oldham Athletic (a) 0–0
4th Round Replay – Oldham Athletic (h) 0–1

1994/95
3rd Round – Bristol City (a) 0–0
3rd Round Replay – Bristol City (h) 1–3

1995/96
3rd Round – Nottingham Forest (h) 1–1
3rd Round Replay – Nottingham Forest (a) 0–2

1996/97
3rd Round – Stockport County (h) 0–2

1997/98
3rd Round – West Bromwich Albion (a) 1–3

1998/99
1st Round – Reading (a) 1–0
2nd Round – Swansea City (a) 0–1

1999/00
1st Round – Blackpool (a) 0–2

2000/01
1st Round – Nuneaton Borough (h) 0–0
1st Round Replay – Nuneaton Borough (a) 0–1

2001/02
1st Round – Lewes (a) 2–0 (at the Britannia Stadium)
2nd Round – Halifax Town (a) 1–1
2nd Replay – Halifax Town (h) 3–0
3rd Round – Everton (h) 0–1

2002/03
3rd Round – Wigan Athletic (h) 3–0
4th Round – Bournemouth (h) 3–0
5th Round – Chelsea (h) 0–2

2003/04
3rd Round – Wimbledon (a) 1–1
3rd Round Replay – Wimbledon (h) 0–1

2004/05
3rd Round – Arsenal (a) 1–2

2005/06
3rd Round – Tamworth (h) 0–0
3rd Round Replay – Tamworth (a) 1–1 (won 5–4 on
    penalties)
4th Round – Walsall (h) 2–1
5th Round – Birmingham City (h) 0–1

2006/07
3rd Round – Millwall (h) 2–0
4th Round – Fulham (a) 0–3

2007/08
3rd Round – Newcastle United (h) 0–0
3rd Round Replay – Newcastle United (a) 1–4

2008/09
3rd Round – Hartlepool United (a) 0–2

2009/10
3rd Round – York City (h) 3–1
4th Round – Arsenal (h) 3–1
5th Round – Man City (h) 3–1
6th Round – Chelsea (a) 0–2

2010/11
3rd Round – Cardiff City (a) 2–0
4th Round – Wolves (a) 1–0
5th Round – Brighton (h) 3–0
6th Round – West Ham (h) 2–1
Semi-final – Bolton (n) 5–0
Final – Man City (n) 0–1

2011/12
3rd Round – Gillingham (a) 3–1
4th Round – Derby County (a) 2–0
5th Round – Crawley (a) 2–0
6th Round – Liverpool (a) 1–2

THANKS BURY MUCH!

City's most epic FA Cup tussle occurred during the 1954/55 campaign when it took FIVE matches to settle a third-round clash with Bury. The first tie took place on 8 January at Gigg Lane and ended 1–1. The replay at the Victoria Ground also ended 1–1, meaning a neutral venue was needed.

The teams travelled to Goodison Park for a third meeting in ten days, only to share a six-goal thriller. Then it was across the city of Liverpool to Anfield for a third replay, but again the two sides could not be separated after drawing 2–2.

The fifth, and ultimately decisive clash, was played at Old Trafford and this time the Potters emerged victorious, winning 3–2 having played five games in just 17 days!

Ironically, the teams had met twice in three days in the League just a fortnight earlier, with City winning 3–2 at home on Christmas Day and then – surprise, surprise – drawing 1–1 at Gigg Lane two days later, making a total of seven meetings in the space of a month!

PUT THE SUITS BACK, LADS …

Arsenal twice denied City the glamour of successive FA Cup finals after successive semi-final triumphs in 1971 and 1972. One of City's best teams of the modern era were desperately unlucky to play the Gunners at the same stage for two seasons running but on each occasion, Tony Waddington's side gave their all in a bid to make history.

For the first semi-final meeting in '71, City had every right to believe they had the edge as they had already beaten Arsenal 5–0 at the Victoria Ground earlier that season. When the Potters raced into a 2–0 lead at Hillsborough, it seemed Wembley was finally beckoning.

Both goals were farcical from an Arsenal perspective with Peter Storey's clearance bouncing into the net off Denis Smith and John Ritchie capitalising on Charlie George's poor backpass. Arguably the turning point came when Jimmy Greenhoff fluffed a golden chance to put City 3–0 up before half time. It was to give Arsenal the glimmer of hope they needed and after Storey made it 2–1, Frank McLintock met George Armstrong's cross with a firm header which beat Gordon Banks, only to see a certain goal palmed away by John Mahoney. Penalty! Storey then stroked the ball home for a stoppage-time equaliser and goals from George Graham and Kennedy saw off City four days later in Birmingham.

Arsenal went on to win the League and FA Cup double. The following season Arsenal repeated the feat, though it was City who came from behind in the first semi-final to draw 1–1 and force a replay, though the Gunners again emerged victorious with a 2–1 victory at Goodison Park. Of course, the long wait finally ended in 2010 when the Potters took on Manchester City in the final, though Yaya Touré's goal proved enough to give the Blues victory and end their own 34-year wait for a major trophy.

THIRD PLACE PLAY-OFF

As a footnote to the above matches, the FA were experimenting at the time with the two losing semi-finalists meeting for a third-place play-off. It's hard to imagine the apathy the idea generated, but City dutifully took place in the farcical idea by first playing Everton the night before the 1971 FA Cup final (at Selhurst Park).

Around 5,000 fans bothered turning up for the game which actually turned out to be quite entertaining with City coming from 2–0 down to win 3–2 thanks to goals from Terry Conroy and a late brace from John Ritchie. City then took on Birmingham City in August 1972, losing the latter 4–3 on penalties – the first FA Cup tie to ever be settled this way.

RECORD BREAKERS

The all-conquering Leeds United side arrived at the Victoria Ground in February 1975, still unbeaten and nine points clear at the top of Division One.

City were languishing in sixteenth, just above the relegation zone, but had already taken a point off of the champions-elect earlier in the campaign following a 1–1 draw at Elland Road. Looking to make it 30 games without defeat, City won 3–2 and embarked on a run that would see them finish in fifth position and earn UEFA Cup qualifcation. Leeds, meanwhile, won just one of their next six games but still went on to claim the title.

WRITE ON!

Two Stoke City footballers have received the prestigious Football Writers' Footballer of the Year Award while playing for the club.

Sir Stanley Matthews was the first recipient for his displays during the 1962/63 campaign (he'd already won it in 1947/48 for Blackpool and also been voted European Footballer of the Year in 1956 while with the Tangerines).

Gordon Banks was bestowed with the honour in 1972 after a stunning season in goal.

BANKSY SAID IT …
QUOTES FROM A LIVING LEGEND

'The people of Stoke-on-Trent have been absolutely marvellous to myself and my family. I do really feel like an adopted son now.'

**The England legend at the unveiling
of his statue (2008)**

'At that level, every goal is like a knife in the ribs.'

Gordon, on life with England

'That save from Pelé's header was the best I ever made. I didn't have any idea how famous it would become – to start with, I didn't even realise I'd made it at all.'

Banksy – a genius and he didn't know it!

'I've met Pelé several times since that day and he always mentions that save and gives me an affectionate hug and a smile.'

Banks and Pelé's mutual admiration society

'In my early days, a goal against us was shrugged off. Nobody liked conceding a goal, but once the ball had gone into the net it was accepted as "one of those things" and everybody in the team would concentrate on trying to get the goal back. But once the maximum wage had been lifted and win bonuses became all-important, it was suddenly considered a crime to concede a goal.'

Gordon bemoans the lack of joy in top-flight football

YOU BEAUTY!

Since 2003, City have awarded a 'Goal of the Season' trophy to the best strike of the season. Out of the six awards so far, two players have won it twice with Dave Brammer and Ricardo Fuller both winning on successive occasions.

The winners:

2003/04	Peter Hoekstra v Reading (second goal of three scored on day)
2004/05	Dave Brammer v Leicester City
2005/06	Dave Brammer v Luton Town
2006/07	Andy Griffin v Coventry City
2007/08	Ricardo Fuller v Wolves
2008/09	Ricardo Fuller v Aston Villa
2009/10	Ricardo Fuller v West Ham
2010/11	Jon Walters v Bolton
2011/12	Peter Crouch v Man City

A PINT TO PROVE

The Watney Mann Invitation Cup, referred to as simply the Watney Cup, spanned four years at the start of the 1970s. It was held before the start of the season and was contested by the teams which had scored the most goals in each of the four divisions the season before, and which had not been promoted or admitted to one of the European competitions – phew! The competition was so named thanks to a sponsorship deal with the Watney Mann brewery, one of the very first such deals in English football.

The format was innovative and simplisistc and, in many ways, a forerunner for the cup-ties of today. Two clubs from each division took part, making eight entrants in total. The competition was a straight knockout format, each match was a one-off with no replays and was settled with penalty kicks if the teams could not be separated – indeed, the first-ever penalty shoot-out came in the Watney Cup when Manchester United and Hull City locked horns in 1970 – perhaps fittingly, George Best was the first man to take a spot-kick in a penalty shoot-out in Britain. Unlike most other competitions, the final took place at the home ground of one of the finalists, rather than a neutral venue and City's participation was in the competition's final year, 1974. The Potters beat Plymouth Argyle 1–0 at Home Park, then saw off Bristol City 4–1 at the Victoria Ground before beating Hull City in the final, again in front of Potters' fans, 2–0.

THE POTTERS IN THE PLAY-OFFS

City tasted misery in the play-offs four times in a row before finally getting things right in their fifth and – to date – final attempt. In 1991 Stockport triumphed 2–1 over two legs and four years later Leicester City edged two tight encounters 1–0 on aggregate. The 2000 clash with Gillingham saw eight goals scored over two legs, but despite winning the home leg 3–2, City lost 3–0 at the Priestfield Stadium in the return. There was a second successive Division Two heartbreak a year later when Walsall held firm at the Britannia (0–0) but then romped home 4–2 in the return. Just when the City fans thought they couldn't stomach anymore after losing the home leg 2–1 to Cardiff City, the boys pulled off a terrific 2–0 win at Ninian Park to earn the right to return to Cardiff to take on Brentford at the Millennium Stadium. Goals from Deon Burton and a Ben Burgess own goal gave City a 2–0 win and promotion to Division One, now the Championship. The complete record is:

1991/1992

Date	Level	Opposition	Venue	Res
10/5/1992	Div 3 (old)	Stockport County	A	0–1
13/5/1992	Div 3 (old)	Stockport County	H	1–1

Stoke lose 1–2 on aggregate

1995/1996

Date	Level	Opposition	Venue	Res
12/5/1996	Div 1	Leicester City	A	0–0
15/5/1996	Div 1	Leicester City	H	0–1

Stoke lose 0–1 on aggregate

1999/2000

Date	Level	Opposition	Venue	Res
13/5/2000	Div 2	Gillingham	H	3–2
17/5/2000	Div 2	Gillingham	A	0–3 (aet)

Stoke lose 3–5 on aggregate

2000/2001

Date	Level	Opposition	Venue	Res
13/5/2001	Div 2	Walsall	H	0–0
16/5/2001	Div 2	Walsall	A	2–4

Stoke lose 2–4 on aggregate

2001/2002

Date	Level	Opposition	Venue	Res
28/4/2002	Div 2	Cardiff City	H	1–2
01/5/2002	Div 2	Cardiff City	A	2–0

Stoke win 3–2 on aggregate

11/5/2002   p/o final   Brentford City   N   2–0
Venue: Millennium Stadium
Attendance: 42,523
Referee: Graham Laws
Stoke promoted to Division One

Total play-off record:
Pld 11   W 4   D 3   L 4   F 11   A 14

LEAGUE CUP: COMPLETE RECORD

1960/61
2nd Round – Doncaster Rovers (a) 1–3

1961/62
1st Round – Southend United (a) 1–0
2nd Round – Charlton Athletic (a) 1–4

1962/63
2nd Round – Walsall (a) 2–1
3rd Round – Aston Villa (a) 1–3

1963/64
2nd Round – Scunthorpe United (a) 2–2
2nd Round Replay – Scunthorpe United (h) 3–3
2nd Round 2nd Replay – Scunthorpe United (n) 1–0 (at
    Hillsborough)
3rd Round – Bolton Wanderers (h) 3–0
4th Round – Bournemouth & Boscombe Athletic (h)
    2–1
Quarter-Final – Rotherham United (h) 3–2
Semi-Final 1st Leg – Manchester City (h) 2–0
Semi-Final 2nd Leg – Manchester City (a) 0–1 (won 2–1
    on aggregate)

Final 1st Leg – Leicester City (h) 1–1
Final 2nd Leg – Leicester City (a) 2–3 (lost 3–4 on
    aggregate)

1964/65
2nd Round – Shrewsbury Town (h) 1–1
2nd Round Replay – Shrewsbury Town (a) 1–0
3rd Round – Southend United (h) 3–1
4th Round – Plymouth Argyle (h) 1–1
4th Round Replay – Plymouth Argyle (a) 1–3

1965/66
2nd Round – Norwich City (h) 2–1
3rd Round – Chesterfield (a) 2–2
3rd Round Replay – Chesterfield (h) 2–1
4th Round – Burnley (h) 0–0
4th Round Replay – Burnley (a) 1–2

1966/67
2nd Round – Walsall (a) 1–2

1967/68
2nd Round – Watford (h) 2–0
3rd Round – Ipswich Town (h) 2–1
4th Round – Sheffield Wednesday (a) 0–0
4th Round Replay – Sheffield Wednesday (h) 2–1
Quarter-Final – Leeds United (a) 0–2

1968/69
2nd Round – Blackburn Rovers (a) 1–1
2nd Round Replay – Blackburn Rovers (h) 0–1

1969/70
2nd Round – Burnley (h) 0–2

1970/71
2nd Round – Millwall (h) 0–0
2nd Round Replay – Millwall (a) 1–2

1971/72
2nd Round – Southport (a) 2–1
3rd Round – Oxford United (a) 1–1
3rd Round Replay – Oxford United (h) 2–0
4th Round – Manchester United (a) 1–1
4th Round Replay – Manchester United (h) 0–0
4th Round 2nd Replay – Manchester United (h) 2–1
Quarter-Final – Bristol Rovers (a) 4–2
Semi-Final 1st Leg – West Ham United (h) 1–2
Semi-Final 2nd Leg – West Ham United (a) 1–0 (draw
    2–2 on aggregate)
Semi-Final Replay – West Ham United (n) 0–0 (at
    Hillsborough)
Semi-Final 2nd Replay – West Ham United (n) 3–2 (at
    Old Trafford)
Final – Chelsea (n) 2–1 (at Wembley)

1972/73
2nd Round – Sunderland (h) 3–0
3rd Round – Ipswich Town (a) 2–1
4th Round – Notts County (a) 1–3

1973/74
2nd Round – Chelsea (h) 1–0
3rd Round – Middlesbrough (h) 1–1
3rd Round Replay – Middlesbrough (a) 2–1
4th Round – Coventry City (a) 1–2

1974/75
2nd Round – Halifax Town (h) 3–0
3rd Round – Chelsea (a) 2–2
3rd Round Replay – Chelsea (h) 1–1

3rd Round 2nd Replay – Chelsea (h) 6–2
4th Round – Ipswich Town (a) 1–2

1975/76
2nd Round – Lincoln City (a) 1–2

1976/77
2nd Round – Leeds United (h) 2–1
3rd Round – Newcastle United (a) 0–3

1977/78
2nd Round – Bristol City (a) 0–1

1978/79
2nd Round – Sunderland (a) 2–0
3rd Round – Northampton Town (a) 3–1
4th Round – Charlton Athletic (a) 3–2
Quarter-Final – Watford (h) 0–0
Quarter-Final Replay – Watford (a) 1–3

1979/80
2nd Round 1st Leg – Swansea City (h) 1–1
2nd Round 2nd Leg – Swansea City (a) 3–1 (won 4–2
    on aggregate)
3rd Round – Swindon Town (h) 2–2
3rd Round Replay – Swindon Town (a) 1–2

1980/81
2nd Round 1st Leg – Manchester City (h) 1–1
2nd Round 2nd Leg – Manchester City (a) 0–3 (lost 4–1
    on aggregate)

1981/82 – The Milk Cup
2nd Round 1st Leg – Manchester City (a) 0–2
2nd Round 2nd Leg – Manchester City (h) 2–0 (drew
    2–2 on aggregate, lost 8–9 on penalties)

1982/83 – The Milk Cup
2nd Round 1st Leg – West Ham United (h) 1–1
2nd Round 2nd Leg – West Ham United (a) 1–2 (lost
    2–3 on aggregate)

1983/84 – The Milk Cup
2nd Round 1st Leg – Peterborough United (h) 0–0
2nd Round 2nd Leg – Peterborough United (a) 2–1
    (won 2–1 on aggregate)
3rd Round – Huddersfield Town (h) 0–0
3rd Round Replay – Huddersfield Town (a) 2–0
4th Round – Sheffield Wednesday (h) 0–1

1984/85 – The Milk Cup
2nd Round 1st Leg – Rotherham United (h) 1–2
2nd Round 2nd Leg – Rotherham United (a) 1–1 (lost
    2–3 on aggregate)

1985/86 – The Milk Cup
2nd Round 1st Leg – Wrexham (a) 1–0
2nd Round 2nd Leg – Wrexham (h) 1–0 (won 2–0 on
    aggregate)
3rd Round – Portsmouth (a) 0–2

1986/87 – The Littlewoods Cup
2nd Round 1st Leg – Shrewsbury Town (a) 1–2
2nd Round 2nd Leg – Shrewsbury Town (h) 0–0 (lost
    1–2 on aggregate)

1987/88 – The Littlewoods Cup
2nd Round 1st Leg – Gillingham (h) 2–0
2nd Round 2nd Leg – Gillingham (a) 1–0 (won 3–0 on
    aggregate)
3rd Round – Norwich City (h) 2–1
4th Round – Arsenal (a) 0–3

1988/89 – The Littlewoods Cup
2nd Round 1st Leg – Leyton Orient (a) 2–1
2nd Round 2nd Leg – Leyton Orient (h) 1–2 (drew 3–3
    on aggregate, lost 2–3 on penalties)

1989/90 – The Littlewoods Cup
2nd Round 1st Leg – Millwall (h) 1–0
2nd Round 2nd Leg – Millwall (a) 0–2 (lost 1–2 on
    aggregate)

1990/91 – The Rumbelows Cup
1st Round 1st Leg – Swansea City (h) 0–0
1st Round 2nd Leg – Swansea City (a) 1–0 (won 1–0 on
    aggregate)
2nd Round 1st Leg – West Ham United (a) 0–3
2nd Round 2nd Leg – West Ham United (h) 1–2 (lost
    1–5 on aggregate)

1991/92 – The Rumbelows Cup
1st Round 1st Leg – Chesterfield (h) 1–0
1st Round 2nd Leg – Chesterfield (a) 2–1 (won 3–1 on
    aggregate)
2nd Round 1st Leg – Liverpool (a) 2–2
2nd Round 2nd Leg – Liverpool (h) 2–3 (lost 4–5 on
    aggregate)

1992/93 – The Coca-Cola Cup
1st Round 1st Leg – Preston North End (a) 1–2
1st Round 2nd Leg – Preston North End (h) 4–0 (won
    5–2 on aggregate)
2nd Round 1st Leg – Cambridge United (a) 2–2
2nd Round 2nd Leg – Cambridge United (h) 1–2 (lost
    3–4 on aggregate)

1993/94 – The Coca-Cola Cup
1st Round 1st Leg – Mansfield Town (h) 2–2
1st Round 2nd Leg – Mansfield Town (a) 3–1 (won 5–3
    on aggregate)

2nd Round 1st Leg – Manchester United (h) 2–1
2nd Round 2nd Leg – Manchester United (a) 0–2 (lost
    2–3 on aggregate)

1994/95 – The Coca-Cola Cup
2nd Round 1st Leg – Fulham (a) 2–3
2nd Round 2nd Leg – Fulham (h) 1–0 (drew 3–3 on
    aggregate, won on away goals)
3rd Round – Liverpool (a) 1–2

1995/96 – The Coca-Cola Cup
2nd Round 1st Leg – Chelsea (h) 0–0
2nd Round 2nd Leg – Chelsea (a) 1–0
3rd Round – Newcastle United (h) 0–4

1996/97 – The Coca-Cola Cup
2nd Round 1st Leg – Northampton Town (h) 1–0
2nd Round 2nd Leg – Northampton Town (a) 2–1 (won
    3–1 on aggregate)
3rd Round – Arsenal (h) 1–1
3rd Round Replay – Arsenal (a) 2–5

1997/98 – The Coca-Cola Cup
1st Round 1st Leg – Rochdale (a) 3–1
1st Round 2nd Leg – Rochdale (h) 1–1 (won 4–2 on
    aggregate)
2nd Round 1st Leg – Burnley (a) 4–0
2nd Round 2nd Leg – Burnley (h) 2–0 (won 6–0 on
    aggregate)
3rd Round – Leeds United (h) 1–3

1998/99 – The Worthington Cup
1st Round 1st Leg – Macclesfield Town (a) 1–3
1st Round 2nd Leg – Macclesfield Town (h) 1–0 (lost
    2–3 on aggregate)

1999/2000 – The Worthington Cup
1st Round 1st Leg – Macclesfield Town (a) 1–1
1st Round 2nd Leg – Macclesfield Town (h) 3–0 (won
    4–1 on aggregate)
2nd Round 1st Leg – Sheffield Wednesday (h) 0–0
2nd Round 2nd Leg – Sheffield Wednesday (a) 1–3 (lost
    1–3 on aggregate)

2000/01 – The Worthington Cup
1st Round 1st Leg – York City (a) 5–1
1st Round 2nd Leg – York City (h) 0–0 (won 5–1 on
    aggregate)
2nd Round 1st Leg – Charlton Athletic (h) 2–1
2nd Round 2nd Leg – Charlton Athletic (a) 3–4 (drew
    5–5 on aggregate, won on away goals)
3rd Round – Barnsley (h) 3–2
4th Round – Liverpool (h) 0–8

2001/02 – The Worthington Cup
1st Round – Oldham Athletic (h) 0–0 (lost 5–6 on
    penalties)

2002/03 – The Worthington Cup
1st Round – Bury (a) 0–1

2003/04 – The Carling Cup
1st Round – Rochdale (h) 2–1
2nd Round – Gillingham (h) 0–2

2004/05 – The Carling Cup
1st Round – Oldham Athletic (a) 1–2

2005/06 – The Carling Cup
1st Round – Mansfield Town (a) 1–1 (lost 0–3 on
    penalties)

2006/07 – The Carling Cup
1st Round – Darlington (h) 1–2

2007/08 – The Carling Cup
1st Round – Rochdale (a) 2–2 (lost 2–4 on penalties)

2008/09 – The Carling Cup
2nd Round – Cheltenham Town (a) 3–2
3rd Round – Reading (h) 2–2 (won 4–3 on penalties)
4th Round – Rotherham United (h) 2–0
Quarter-Final – Derby County (h) 0–1

2009/10 – The Carling Cup
2nd Round – Leyton Orient (a) 1–0
3rd Round – Blackpool (h) 4–3
4th Round – Portsmouth (a) 0–4

2010/11 – The Carling Cup
2nd Round – Shrewsbury Town (h) 2–1
3rd Round – Fulham (h) 2–0
4th Round – West Ham (a) 1–3

2011/12 – The Carling Cup
3rd Round – Spurs (h) 0–0 (won 7–6 on penalties)
4th Round – Liverpool (h) 1–2

AT LAST!

The Potters' epic twelve-match journey to the 1971/72 League Cup Final will never be forgotten by those old enough to remember it.

The run included an incredible five replays along the way and saw City see off the likes of West Ham and Manchester United before facing Chelsea at Wembley on 4 March 1972. In front of 100,000 fans, goals from Terry Conroy and a late winner from George Eastham caused what was quite an upset at the time as City finally won their first major trophy.

The star men were Mike Pejic and the brilliant Gordon Banks and the team who wrote their name into the history books that day was: Gordon Banks, John Marsh, Mike Pejic, Mike Bernard, Denis Smith, Alan Bloor, Terry Conroy, Jimmy Greenhoff, John Ritchie, Peter Dobing, George Eastham and the substitute was John Mahoney.

ANGLO-ITALIAN CUP

City have taken part in the Anglo-Italian Cup on four occasions, only once progressing past the group stages. Despite winning two and drawing two of their group games in 1970/71, City were eliminated from the competition by virtue of other teams' performances. Two wins and two defeats in the group stage a year later meant a similar outcome, though the Potters fared better when the competition was revamped in the 1990s, reaching the two-legged semi-final against the mighty Italian outfit Notts County (!) and after two 0–0 draws, the Magpies triumphed 3–2 on penalties. The complete record is:

1970/71
Roma (h) 2–2
Verona (h) 2–0
Roma (a) 1–0
Verona (a) 1–1

1971/72
Cantanzaro (a) 3–0
Roma (a) 0–2
Cantanzaro (h) 2–0
Roma (h) 1–2

1993/94
Group 7 – Wolverhampton Wanderers (a) 3–3
Group 7 – Birmingham City (h) 2–0
Group B – Cosenza (h) 2–1
Group B – Fiorentina (h) 0–0
Group B – Padova (a) 0–3
Group B – Pescara (a) 1–2

1994/95
Group B – Cesena (a) 2–0
Group B – Ancona (h) 1–1
Group B – Udinese (a) 3–1
Group B – Piacenza (h) 4–0
Semi-Final 1st Leg – Notts County (a) 0–0
Semi-Final 2nd Leg – Notts County (h) 0–0*
* Notts County won 3-2 on penalties

ANGLO-SCOTTISH CUP

City's participation in this curious competition, originally
known as the Texaco Cup until the petroleum giants'
withdrawal in 1975, pretty much starts and ends with
Motherwell, with Derby County kind of sandwiched in
between. The first foray across the border in 1970 ended
in a 1–0 defeat to the 'Well, though a 2–1 home victory
at least levelled the aggregate score and forced a penalty
shoot-out. The Scots triumphed 4–3 on spot-kicks but City
gained revenge the following season, during the 1971/72
campaign, with a 1–0 win for the Potters at Fir Park and
a 4–1 stroll at the Victoria Ground. Unfortunately further
progress was halted by fellow Sassenachs Derby County,
who beat City 3–2 at the Baseball Ground and then drew
2–2 in the return leg in Stoke. The Rams went on to win
the competition, beating Aidrieonians 2–1 over two legs.
In 1973/74, City drew Birmingham City over two legs.
The first leg was at the Vic, with no goals to entertain the

sparse crowd and the second leg ended 0–0 at St Andrew's a fortnight later. The Blues won the game on a penalty shoot-out to progress to the second round where they were duly dumped out by Newcastle United. In the all-time Texaco Cup table, the Potters lie thirteenth of 49 teams. The complete record is:

1970/71
Motherwell (a) 0–1
Motherwell (h) 2–1*
* Motherwell won 4–3 on penalties after the scores had finished level over two legs

1971/72
Motherwell (a) 1–0
Motherwell (h) 4–1
Derby County (a) 2–3
Derby County (h) 2–2

1973/74
Birmingham City (h) 0–0
Birmingham City (a) 0–0*
* Birmingham won on penalties

UEFA CUP – EUROPEAN GLORY ... ALMOST!

City's first ever UEFA Cup game against European opposition came in 1972 when they played Kaiserslautern at the Victoria Ground. A stirring display from Tony Waddington's side resulted in a 3–1 victory against the Bundesliga outfit, but the Germans proved a different kettle of fish on their own ground, wiping out the deficit with a 4–1 win to go through 5–4 on aggregate.

City were back in the UEFA Cup two years later but were drawn against former European Cup champions Ajax. The Dutch masters, minus the genius of Barcelona-bound Johan Cruyff, were considered – with some justification – to be one of the greatest clubs in the world and it was going to be a stern test for Waddington's inexperienced side – but one they would emerge from with great credit. The key was not to concede a goal in the home leg, but on 38 minutes, Ajax skipper Ruud Krol turned a difficult tie into a monumental hurdle as he fired home a 20-yard drive past Farmer. City came out with fire in their bellies after the break and Denis Smith levelled scores on 76 minutes and the game ended in a creditable 1–1 draw. The return leg in the Olympic Stadium proved that the Potters had learned a lot from their previous European adventure, but they couldn't find the goal they perhaps deserved on the night and despite an excellent 0–0 draw, they were eliminated.

The Potters made an impressive Europa League debut (the new name for the UEFA Cup) and can consider themselves unlucky not to have progressed further than they finally did. City started in classic European style, beating Hadjuk Split 1–0 home and away to progress 2–0 on aggregate. Jon Walters scored in the home leg and an own goal in injury time completed a win in Split. Then Tony Pulis' men saw off Swiss side Thun with a 1–0 win through Pugh's goal and a 4–1 return win at the Britannia ensured a comfortable passage to the group stages thanks to goals from Upson, Jones (2) and Whelan. Victories over Besiktas and two wins over Maccabi Tel Aviv meant the Potters progressed as group runners-up but a 1–0 defeat at home and away to Valencia ended City's interest in the round of 32.

STAFFORDSHIRE FA SENIOR CUP

One competition of particular interest to City fans is the now-defunct Staffordshire Senior Cup. Unfortunately for City, games against Aston Villa, Wolverhampton Wanderers or West Brom usually ended in defeat (24 occasions in 37 years against all three!). Featuring games against some wonderfully named local teams, here is the complete record – at least of all the traceable matches – of the Potters' SSC results in the competition from which they emerged champions on four occasions.

1877/78
1st Round – Mow Cop (h) 26–0
2nd Round – Hanley Rovers (h) 2–0
3rd Round – Leek (h) 1–0
Semi-Final – Ashbourne (h) 1–0
Final – Talke Rangers (h) 1–0

1878/79
1st Round – Goldenhill (h) 3–0
2nd Round – Leek (a) 2–0
Semi-Final – Talke Rangers (a) 1–0
Final – Cobridge (h) 2–1

1880/81
1st Round – West Bromwich Albion (a) 0–2

1882/83
1st Round – Stoke Priory (h) 19–0
2nd Round – Cocknage (h) 10–0
3rd Round – Leek White Star (h) 7–1
Semi-Final – Burslem Port Vale (a) 1–1
Semi-Final Replay – Burslem Port Vale (h) 5–1
Final – West Bromwich Albion (h) 2–3

1884/85
1st Round – Fenton (h) 12–0
2nd Round – West Bromwich Albion (a) 2–6

1885/86
1st Round – Goldenhill (a) 1–0
2nd Round – Smallthorne (a) 7–1
3rd Round – Mitchell's St George (h) 1–1
3rd Round Replay – Mitchell's St George (h) 2–0
Semi-Final – Walsall Town Swifts (h) 3–1
Final – West Bromwich Albion (a) 2–4

1886/87
1st Round – Biddulph (h) 14–0
2nd Round – Wolverhampton Wanderers (a) 1–3

1887/88
1st Round – Burslem Port Vale (h) 1–0
Semi-Final – West Bromwich Albion (h) 0–1

1888/89
1st Round – Wednesday Old Athletic (a) 3–2
2nd Round – Walsall Town Swifts (a) 0–3

1889/90
1st Round – West Bromwich Albion (a) 0–4

1890/91
1st Round – Burton Swifts (a) 2–1
2nd Round – Aston Villa (n) 1–4

1892/93
1st Round – Aston Villa (a) 1–6

1893/94
1st Round – Burton Swifts (h) 5–4
2nd Round – Wolverhampton Wanderers (h) 0–2

1894/95
1st Round – Wolverhampton Wanderers (h) 1–2

1895/96
1st Round – Burslem Port Vale (a) 4–0
Semi-Final – Burton Wanderers (h) 3–0
Final – Aston Villa (h) 1–1
Final Replay – Aston Villa (a) 0–5

1896/97
1st Round – Burton Swifts (h) 2–1
2nd Round – Dresden United (h) 3–0
Semi-Final – Wolverhampton Wanderers (h) 0–0
Semi-Final Replay – Wolverhampton Wanderers (a) 0–2

1897/98
1st Round – Burton Swifts (h) 3–4*
1st Round Replay – Burton Swifts (h) 4–2
2nd Round – Burslem Port Vale (a) 1–3
* game replayed after protest!

1898/99
1st Round – Burton Swifts (h) 3–1
2nd Round – Aston Villa (a) 1–3

1899/1900
1st Round – West Bromwich Albion (h) 1–3

1900/01
1st Round – Burslem Port Vale (h) 2–0
Semi-Final – Aston Villa (a) 1–1
Semi-Final Replay – Aston Villa (h) 2–0
Final – Wolverhampton Wanderers (a) 1–3

1901/02
1st Round – Burton United (h) 8–0
Semi-Final – Burslem Port Vale (a) 2–1
Final – West Bromwich Albion (n) 0–3

1902/03
1st Round – Burslem Port Vale (a) 1–1
1st Round Replay – Burslem Port Vale (h) 2–0
Semi-Final – Small Heath (h) 1–0
Final – West Bromwich Albion (n) 0–2

1903/04
1st Round – Burslem Port Vale (h) 5–2
Semi-Final – Burton United (h) 5–0
Final – Wolverhampton Wanderers (h) 2–2
Final Replay – Wolverhampton Wanderers (a) 2–2*
* trophy shared

1904/05
1st Round – Burton United (a) 2–2
1st Round Replay – Burton United (h) 8–0
Semi-Final – Small Heath (a) 0–3

1905/06
1st Round – Burslem Port Vale (h) 0–5

1907/08
1st Round – Aston Villa reserves (h) 3–0
2nd Round – Birmingham reserves (a) 0–2

1908/09
1st Round – Aston Villa (a) 0–9

1909/10
1st Round – Burton United (h) 8–1
2nd Round – Aston Villa (a) 1–3

1910/11
1st Round – West Bromwich Albion (h) 3–2
2nd Round – Aston Villa (a) 1–3

1911/12
1st Round – Aston Villa (a) 0–3

1912/13
1st Round – Aston Villa (a) 0–4

1913/14
Semi-Final – West Bromwich Albion (h) 3–1
Final – Walsall (n) 4–2
(Stoke City's reserve and/or youth teams tended to
compete after 1914)

UNITED COUNTIES LEAGUE

City's participation in the UCL involved home and away games against three local teams. They were played during the 1893/94 season and the results were as follows:

1893/94
10 March – West Brom (a) 0–5
17 March – Wolves (a) 2–1
19 March – West Brom (h) 5–2
2 April – Small Heath (a) 0–3
9 April – Small Heath (h) 2–1
16 April – Wolves (h) 3–0

CITY GENTS

The Potters were formed as Stoke Ramblers in 1863 but in 1878, after moving to the Victoria Ground, the fledgling club merged with Stoke Victoria Cricket Club to become Stoke FC – their rambling days clearly over! After becoming a founder member of the Football League in 1888, Stoke lost their League status after finishing bottom for successive seasons but were re-elected in 1891 after winning the Football Alliance a year later. The club was wound up because of increasing financial problems in 1908 and forced to resign from the League, but re-formed the same year with a new board and squad, deciding to field two teams in league competition, one in the Birmingham & District League and the other in the Southern League (West Division). The club won its place back in the Football League in 1915, but the First World War meant League football was suspended and Stoke instead played their wartime football in the Lancashire Primary & Secondary leagues. When war was over, the club returned to League football and, following Stoke-on-Trent gaining city status in 1925, Stoke became Stoke City from then onwards.

OUTCASTS!

Here are the stats for Stoke's time in the Birmingham & District and Southern leagues:

1908/09 – Birmingham & District League Division One
P 34   W 13   D 5   L 16   F 71   A 64   Pts 31
Position 8th

1909/10 – Birmingham & District League Division One
P 34   W 17   D 7   L 10   F 84   A 48   Pts 37
Position 7th

1910/11 – Birmingham & District League Division One
P 34   W 24   D 2   L 8   F 95   A 48   Pts 50
Position 1st

1909/10 – Southern League Qualifying
P 10   W 10   D 0   L 0   F 48   A 9   Pts 20
Position 1st

1910/11 – Southern League Division Two
P 22   W 17   D 1   L 4   F 72   A 20   Pts 35
Position 2nd

1911/12 – Southern League Division One
P 38   W 13   D 10   L 15   F 51   A 63   Pts 36
Position 10th

1912/13 – Southern League Division One
P 38   W 10   D 4   L 24   F 39   A 75   Pts 24
Position 20th

1913/14 – Southern League Division Two
P 30   W 20   D 4   L 6   F 71   A 34   Pts 34
Position 5th

1914/15 – Southern League Division Two
P 24   W 17   D 4   L 3   F 62   A 15   Pts 38
Position 1st

THE ASSOCIATE MEMBERS' CUP/ FOOTBALL LEAGUE TROPHY

The Associate Members' Cup (or Football League Trophy from 1991) has had various sponsors and monikers over the years (six in all during Stoke's participation). It has provided a welcome distraction for City fans during the club's leaner years and has twice resulted in fantastic days out at Wembley, with the Potters winning the trophy on both occasions.

For the first years, the competition included teams from all four divisions until it became the Football League Trophy, catering for teams outside the top two divisions only. In 1992 City beat Stockport County 1–0 to collect the Autoglass Trophy and in 2000 returned to beat Bristol City 2–1 and land the Auto Windscreens Shield. The Potters' complete record is:

1985/86 – Full Members' Cup
Group Three South – Coventry City (h) 3–0
Group Three South – Millwall (a) 2–2
Semi-Final South – Oxford United (h) 0–1

1986/87 – Freight Rover Trophy/ Full Members' Cup
1st Round – Sheffield United (h) 1–2

1987/88 – Sherpa Van Trophy/Full Members' Cup
1st Round – Portsmouth (a) 3–0
2nd Round – Sheffield Wednesday (a) 1–0
3rd Round – Leicester City (a) 0–0 (won 5–3 on penalties)
Quarter-Final – Luton Town (a) 1–4

1988/89 – Sherpa Van Trophy/Full Members' Cup
1st Round – Southampton (a) 0–3

1989/90 – Leyland DAF Trophy/Full Members' Cup
2nd Round North – Bradford City (h) 2–1
Quarter-Final North – Leeds United (h) 2–2 (lost 4–5 on
    penalties)

1990/91 – Leyland DAF Trophy/Full Members' Cup
Group 4 South – Mansfield Town (a) 0–3
Group 4 South – Northampton Town (h) 1–1

*1991/92 – Autoglass Trophy/Football League Trophy
    1991 onwards*
Group 5 South – Walsall (a) 2–0
Group 5 South – Birmingham City (h) 3–1
1st Round South – Cardiff City (h) 3–0
Quarter–Finals South – Walsall (h) 3–1
Semi-Final South – Leyton Orient (a) 1–0
Final South 1st Leg – Peterborough United (h) 3–3
Final South 2nd Leg – Peterborough United (a) 1–0
Final – Stockport County (n) 1–0 (at Wembley)

1998/99 – Auto Windscreens Shield
1st Round North – Blackpool (a) 2–0
2nd Round North – Rochdale (a) 1–2 (at the Britannia
    Stadium)

1999/2000 – Auto Windscreens Shield
1st Round North – Darlington (h) 3–2
2nd Round North – Oldham Athletic (a) 1–0
Quarter-Final North – Blackpool (a) 2–1
Semi-Final North – Chesterfield (a) 1–0
Final North 1st Leg – Rochdale (a) 3–1
Final North 2nd Leg – Rochdale (h) 1–0
Final – Bristol City (n) 2–1 (at Wembley)

2000/01 – LDV Vans Trophy
1st Round North – Scarborough (h) 3–1
2nd Round North – Halifax Town (a) 3–2

Quarter-Final North – Walsall (h) 4–0
Semi-Final North – Port Vale (a) 1–2

2001/02 – LDV Vans Trophy
1st Round North – Blackpool (a) 2–3

THE CORONATION LOVING CUP

The Coronation Loving Cup was presented to clubs in 1937 by then Stoke City President – Sir Francis Joseph – to commemorate the coronation of King George VI and Queen Elizabeth on 12 May 1937. The cups were presented to the 22 English First Division clubs who finished the 1936/37 season and to the two clubs that were promoted into the division to start the 1937/38 season.

They were also presented to the Scottish Football Association on the occasion of Britain v Rest of Europe match at Hampden Park, and also to Glasgow Rangers as a tribute to their generosity when they came to Stoke to play a match which added £2,000 to the Holditch Colliery Disaster Fund. The cups were also presented to the English Football Association, the English Football League and to the king himself.

Sir Francis Joseph requested that the cup be used to drink to the health of the reigning monarch on the occasion of the first home match of the New Year.

THE COLOMBIAN CONNECTION

In the 1950s, a rebel group of English footballers left the country to seek better wages and living standards in Colombia. Of these 'revolutionaries', City players George Mountford and Neil Franklin were included. Franklin had been seeking a move away from Stoke for some time – he thought the endless smoke, fumes and smog from the local kilns were unhealthy conditions for him and his family to live in.

When the club refused his transfer requests, he opted to join a steady number of migrants who joined Independiente Santa Fé of Bogotá whose status was outside the jurisdiction of FIFA and therefore considered a rebel organisation; any player who played for them ran the risk of a ban from their own FA. Franklin had 37 England caps to his name and further angered the Football Association by refusing to join up with the England squad for the 1950 World Cup in Brazil – had he played, he would have been Stoke City's first World Cup international player.

Political turmoil in Colombia made it increasingly hard for English players to settle and within a year, most had left. Franklin returned to England but his international career was in shreds and he signed for Hull City. Mountford stayed in America for a year while his ban from English football was in effect and returned to the Potters to continue his career.

THE GAFFERS

Tom Slaney: August 1874 – May 1883
The first official manager of the club, Slaney had previously played for the club from 1871. He continued playing while also being in charge of team affairs. Upon retiring, he became a referee and was also the first chairman of the Staffordshire Football Association.

Walter Cox: June 1883 – April 1884
Cox enjoyed a short period in charge of the club. The only distinction which he managed, was the fact that he was at the helm when Stoke played in their first FA Cup tie in the 1883/84 season.

Harry Lockett: April 1884 – August 1890
Lockett was in charge for the club's first two seasons in the Football League, but overall was the manager for over six years. He represented Stoke at the inaugural meeting of the FA. However, this meeting was not all positive for Stoke, as Lockett was given the job of Secretary of the FA and two years later left the Potteries to concentrate on the job on a full-time basis at the Football Association.

Joseph Bradshaw: August 1890 – January 1892
For their opening season following failure to gain re-election to the Football League, Stoke employed Joseph Bradshaw to take them through a year in the Alliance League, before the club was voted back into the League. Bradshaw left in January 1892 with the side struggling.

Arthur Reeves: January 1892 – May 1895
In the first year of his reign, Reeves guided the Potters to finish seventh in the League. He continued to inspire a gradual progression up the league, by gaining a mid-table position in the next season, and then a highest ever finish of seventh in the 1893/94 campaign before leaving in 1895.

William Rowley: May 1895 – August 1897
Rowley had an interesting career as a professional footballer, starting off as a centre-forward, but ending up playing between the sticks under the stewardship of Arthur Reeves. As the main man, Rowley did little worthy of note, and upon leaving football he became a postman and a landlord before emigrating to the USA.

Horace Austerberry: September 1897 – May 1908
Austerberry took the reins of Stoke and kept hold of them for 11 (generally lean) years. Austerberry was never given sufficient funds to permit any real improvement in the team's fortunes and his most notable success was an FA Cup semi-final in 1899 in which Derby County triumphed 3–1. Unfortunately, in 1908 the club went bust. At this point Austerberry returned to his first love, that of journalism, in order to support his family and write about the perils of managing a skint football team!

Alfred Barker: May 1908 – April 1914
Barker arrived at the Victoria Ground as a saviour, being a member of a consortium hoping to propel the club back into the Football League following their recent demise. Unfortunately, the club was refused immediate re-election to Division Two and were forced to battle in the Birmingham District and Southern Leagues in order to survive. Barker resigned from his position at Stoke in acrimonious circumstances due to an argument regarding his part-time role as secretary at the club.

Peter Hodge: June 1914 – April 1915
Hodge moved from north of the border after a golden period with Raith Rovers which brought him to the attention of the hierarchy at the club. His time at Stoke was cut short due to the outbreak of the First World War, and the subsequent suspension of the Football League calendar. He spent the war years back in his native Scotland and upon the culmination of the conflict, Hodge came back to England where he took charge of Leicester and later Manchester City.

Joseph Schofield: April 1915 – February 1919
A former Stoke player, Schofield was given the task of running team affairs during the First World War. He had previously been a left winger, and was even capped

three times for England in his career. Owing to the circumstances surrounding Britain at the time, his time as manager had minimal impact on the club.

Arthur Shallcross: February 1919 – March 1923
Shallcross led the club in their first season back in the Football League in 1919, and guided the team to promotion in 1922 after finishing runners-up in the Division Two. His side could not challenge in the top flight, and the Potters only had one season back in the Division One before being relegated. Shallcross then left Stoke, even though he had a reasonably competent time as manager. He never took up another job in football management.

John Rutherford: March 1923 – April 1923
Rutherford had only a slight impact on the history of the club, but all for negative reasons. The man from Northumberland had played as a winger of some quality for Newcastle and Woolwich Arsenal. With minimal explanation, Rutherford left Stoke for Arsenal only a few weeks after his appointment as player-manager.

Tom Mather: October 1923 – June 1935
Tom Mather's experience in football before being named as manager of Stoke was as assistant-secretary at both Manchester City and Bolton. At the latter, he was given the task of managing the team, which he did before moving on to Southend. He endured a difficult start in the Potteries following his appointment in 1923, when issues involving the players and their wages eventually resulted in relegation to the Third Division (North). Luckily, he then turned the fortunes of the club around, gained successive promotions and claimed the Division Two title along the way. He stabilised the club in the First Division before departing to take up a similar role at Newcastle and, later, Leicester and Kilmarnock.

However, Mather's credit and reputation will always be good in Stoke – he was, after all, the man who gave Stanley Matthews his debut.

Bob McGrory: June 1935 – May 1952
A Stoke legend in his own right; McGrory joined the club as a player in 1921 after short spells at Dumbarton and Burnley. This was the start of a long career for McGrory in the Potteries, as he went on to make more than 500 appearances for the club and continued his career into his forties. He first retired in order to become the reserve team manager, but owing to injuries, boss Tom Mather asked him to return to playing, which he did and was an ever-present in the side. He played his last match at the age of 42. In 1935 he became the manager of City, and quickly made an impact when the club finished fourth in the First Division. The Second World War then broke out, football was shelved and the chances of success for Stoke went with it. McGrory left in 1952, and ended his managerial career at Merthyr Tydfil.

Frank Taylor: June 1952 – June 1960
Yorkshireman Frank Taylor enjoyed a decent career with Wolves and played in the 1939 FA Cup Final and during the war years. He also represented England before injury forced him to retire in1944. He had a couple of jobs in the role of assistant manager before stepping into his first full managerial job at Stoke. He based his style on a brutal fitness regime but this failed to make an impact and the club were soon relegated. Despite a lack of tangible success, Taylor remained in the post until 1960.

Tony Waddington: June 1960 – February 1977
The legendary, Tony Waddington was promoted from the role as Frank Taylor's assistant to become boss in 1960. In the club's centenary season, Waddington took the Potters back to the First Division, having

won the Division Two title after just two years in charge. Waddington then created a solid side that could compete at the top level, building an excellent squad and turning City into something of a specialist cup team. They reached two FA Cup semi-finals and won the League Cup (in 1972) during his reign, but in 1977, he decided to resign after the club forced him to sell off his better players for financial reasons. His next role in management came at Crewe Alexandra for two seasons. He was appointed to the Stoke City board in 1993, as an associate director – a role which he kept until his death the following year. Only today can his immense achievements for the Potters be fully understood, and he will always be fondly remembered by the club and its supporters.

George Eastham OBE: February 1977 – January 1978
George Eastham played in the 1972 League Cup win, and scored the winning goal to boot. A great servant for Newcastle United and Arsenal, Eastham was a member of the 1966 England World Cup squad, though he failed to play any part in it. Alas, his managerial career could not live up to his playing career. He managed the club for only 11 months, took the club down in his first six months and then failed to mount a serious promotion challenge in the following season. His goal, however, won the club its only major silverware so his credit is always good in Stoke.

Alan Durban: January 1978 – June 1981
Durban was brought in from Shrewsbury Town after gaining a promising reputation in management. During his spell at Gay Meadow, Durban was known as a stern – even dour – character, who had learnt his trade under the guidance of Brian Clough where he played in the championship-winning team at Derby County. He was also capped 27 times by Wales during his playing days.

His first full season in charge led to promotion back to the Division One, and two more of stability in the top flight. When his contract ran out in 1981, he left the Potteries in order to take over at Sunderland. He returned to Stoke in 1998 as assistant to Chic Bates.

Richie Barker: June 1981 – December 1983

Brought in on the recommendation of Alan Durban, Barker succeeded his former boss after periods working at Shrewsbury and Wolves. At Stoke he built a side that continually progressed and was aided by some astute signings such as Sammy McIlroy and Mickey Thomas. Sadly, after the early promise that the team showed, Barker resigned after a poor start to the 1983/84 season.

Bill Asprey: December 1983 – April 1985

Asprey served Stoke with distinction as a player, but his return as a manager is less fondly thought of. He successfully kept the club up in his first season at the club but followed it with a miserable season that ended with the club finishing bottom of the First Division after amassing a record low points total. Asprey failed to see out the season owing to ill health.

Mick Mills MBE: May 1985 – November 1989

As a player, Mick Mills had a great reputation as a solid, dependable full-back with Ipswich Town. He was also the England captain for a time and his first season as player-manager saw City finish mid-table in the Second Division.

A poor financial situation meant that he was unable to bring in many reinforcements and so spent a lot of his time wheeling and dealing. When he was given money, things seemed to take a turn for the worse and Mills was sacked following a 6–0 defeat against Swindon Town in 1989.

Alan Ball: November 1989 – February 1991

The World Cup winner never repeated his success as a player in management. His first season saw City slip into the Third Division and Ball failed to sustain a challenge for promotion the following campaign.

He left partway through the 1990/91 season and his managerial career thereafter included spells with Exeter, Portsmouth and Southampton. He then endured a dismal time in charge at Manchester City, taking them down to Division One.

Lou Macari: May 1991 – October 1993 & October 1994 – May 1997

A former Manchester United player and Scotland international, Macari arrived hoping that success during his playing career could inspire City to promotion. This was nearly achieved in the first year of his reign as he took the club to the play-offs, but no further. This blow was softened slightly by a trip to Wembley where the Potters won the Auto Windscreen Shield.

Macari's team went on to win the Division Three title in 1993. This achievement brought him to the attention of Celtic, for whom he left to take charge of in October 1993. Macari returned to City a year later to spend a further two-and-a-half years at the helm, taking the club to the Division One play-offs in 1996 only to lose out to Leicester City. Macari left in 1997 and still lives in the Stoke-on-Trent area.

Joe Jordan: November 1993 – September 1994

Another ex-Manchester United legend, Joe Jordan adopted a defensive style that never really excited the City fans. In his first season he almost took the Potters to the play-offs, but just fell short, mainly owing to a lack of goals! A poor start to the 1994/95 campaign saw Jordan lose his job – that plus the fact the popular Macari was available again. In recent years the former

AC Milan player has worked under Harry Redknapp, after calling time on his own managerial career.

Chic Bates: July 1997 – January 1998
The brand new Britannia Stadium brought with it a new boss – Chic Bates. Unfortunately, his time at the club lasted a mere six months after he was sacked for a series of poor performances.

Chris Kamara: January 1998 – April 1998
The tough-tackling former Stoke midfielder endured a nigh-on hopeless spell in charge, winning just one of the 14 matches that he oversaw, and taking the club to brink of relegation. His failure in the Potteries was a shock to many, after he had proved a great success with Bradford City. He left after barely three months in charge and is now a popular commentator on Sky Sports.

Brian Little: June 1998 – June 1999
The arrival of Little was a coup for the club considering that six months earlier he'd been in charge of Premiership Aston Villa. Little enjoyed a good start to life at the Britannia, guiding City to the top of the table until mid-December. At the end of the campaign the side had slumped to eighth and Little left the club citing personal reasons as the reason for his departure. Further jobs came his way, but he never reached the heights he enjoyed with Villa, and his most recent role was at Wrexham, which he left in 2008 while they were in the Blue Square Premier.

Gary Megson: July 1999 – November 1999
That Megson only managed a few months at the helm was hardly his own fault – it was simply down to the fact that the club's new Icelandic consortium wanted to bring in their own man. Megson's CV included a long list of clubs during his playing career as well as successful

managerial stints at both Norwich and Stockport. Following his departure from Stoke, he has had spells at West Brom and Nottingham Forest. Megson even returned to the Britannia Stadium to help out Tony Pulis as part of his backroom staff in 2007 before resuming his career as boss of Premier League Bolton Wanderers.

Gudjon Thordarsson: November 1999 – May 2002
The 'Iceman' came in 1999 following a spell as manager of his native Iceland, which almost led to qualification for Euro 2000. Thordarsson built his reputation in his homeland by winning the national championship, and domestic cup competition on many occasions. His time at Stoke was one of near misses with his team making it into the play-offs, but failing to gain promotion. On a positive note, City won the Auto Windscreens Shield in 2000 and promotion to Division One was finally achieved in 2002 following a play-off final victory over Brentford – Thordarsson then left the club.

Steve Cotterill: May 2002 – October 2002
For a man who spent the majority of his playing career as an amateur, Cotterill made a successful transition into League management. His first job was with Irish side Sligo Rovers prior to him returning to his hometown club, Cheltenham Town. This was a golden era of his career, as he brought them three promotions in four years taking them from non-League to the Second Division. Cotterill, however, only survived a few months at Stoke after accepting an offer to be right-hand man to Howard Wilkinson at Sunderland, perhaps with the hope that he was being groomed to one day take over the Black Cats. A dismal season ensued, and both men left their jobs. Luckily, Cotterill was then offered the manager's job at Burnley where he was to stay for five years, before resigning in November 2007.

Tony Pulis: November 2002 – June 2005
Pulis arrived for his first period at Stoke in 2002, following a spell out of the game after being Portsmouth manager.

He showed promise in his early managerial career at Gillingham where he guided them to the Division Two play-off final, only for the Gills to famously lose on penalties to Manchester City after being 2–0 up with 89 minutes played. His first task at Stoke was to avoid relegation, something which he did comfortably. After his grounding at the club, Pulis built a solid outfit that could compete in the newly marketed Championship, though he left at the end of the 2005 campaign to manage Plymouth.

Johan Boskamp: June 2005 – June 2006
A well-travelled manager, Boskamp worked all over the world with success. A former Dutch international, he gained most of his trophies in Belgium managing the likes of Anderlecht and Lierse. He only spent a year at Stoke, but became a popular figure during his time with the club, but just as Gary Megson had been several years earlier, he was a victim of the club being taken over.

Tony Pulis: June 2006–
When Peter Coates gained control of the club, there was only one man who he wanted to lead the team – Tony Pulis.

Pulis left Plymouth Argyle in order to return to Stoke-on-Trent and managed to attract quality players to the club in his first season back. Lee Hendrie and Patrik Berger were brought in on short-term loans to improve the quality of the squad, but the team still missed out on the play-offs.

Against the odds, the Welshman then guided the Potters to the runners-up spot in the Championship and subsequent promotion to the Premier League for the first time. With a collection of shrewd signings, the club easily survived at England's top table of football finishing twelfth, further enhancing Pulis's reputation as a manager of some talent.

Pulis then guided the Potters to the 2011 FA Cup final, took his team into Europe and ensured they finished comfortably in mid-table in 2010, 2011 and 2012 as well as establishing City as a cup team of some note – all in all a tremendous achievement from this determined and studious manager – one of the club's best, in fact.

MAKING A MARK

Popular winger Mark Chamberlain began his career with rivals Port Vale but joined City in August 1982, along with Mark Harrison, for a combined fee of £180,000. When Chamberlain was asked if the move caused him to receive any stick from his mates, he replied, 'No, not really. Mind you I wouldn't, I didn't really have any mates!'

He stayed at the Victoria Ground until September 1985, enjoying three years of sterling service and becoming a huge crowd favourite in the process. A dazzling winger, the ease with which he beat defenders was a thing of beauty. He later joined Sheffield Wednesday before transferring to Portsmouth in 1988. He played 167 games over six years before moving on to Brighton & Hove Albion in August 1994 and ended his playing career with Exeter in 1997.

Chamberlain broke into the England squad under Bobby Robson during his first season at Stoke, scoring on his debut against Luxembourg on 15 December 1982, at the age of 21. He picked up a further seven caps over the next two years and many City fans believe he should have won many more

In April 2008, he accepted an offer to become the assistant coach of the East Timor national football team before returning to England in September 2008 to join the coaching staff at Portsmouth.

His son, Alex Oxlade-Chamberlain, is keeping up family traditions and after establishing himself at Southampton, he won a big-money transfer to Arsenal and has already won senior England recognition.

GROUNDS

Victoria Cricket Club
This was the first setting for Stoke encounters, as their inaugural match was played there in 1868 against the E.W. May XV, in a fifteen-a-side game no less! At this point, the team played under the name Stoke Ramblers, an identity they kept until they merged with the cricket club itself in 1878 when they became Stoke FC.

Sweetings Field
An uninspiring piece of land that was owned by (and named after) the Lord Mayor of the town at the time, Alderman Sweeting. Stoke moved their homes games to the venue, because their previous ground, the Victoria Cricket Ground, was unable to cope with rising crowd numbers. It staged the Potters' matches for three seasons from 1875–8.

Victoria Ground
The home of Stoke City for an impressive 119 years, the Victoria Ground will always hold a place in the hearts of Potters fans. The first game played at the ground was in 1878 when Stoke took on Talke Rangers – the hosts edging a narrow 1–0 win. The Taylor Report's recommendation that all Football League stadia needed to be updated and preferably all-seater affairs, effectively sealed the Victoria Ground's fate and the club instead decided to move to a brand new venue. In its time, the ground witnessed great occasions; the highest attendance came when an estimated 56,000 came to see the centenary game of the club in 1963, when the might of Real Madrid came to town. In celebration of the floodlights installation in the 1950s, Stoke hosted games against Radnicki of Yugoslavia and Essen of Germany. Since the bulldozers razed the ground to rubble, the area

has failed to be redeveloped and, therefore, is currently wasteland – here are some facts and figures:

Facts in brief:

Nickname: The Vic

Inauguration: 28 March 1878 (in use for 119 years)

Originally Named: Athletic Club Ground, renamed the Victoria Ground after the Victoria Hotel which was built on the nearby Sweetings Field

Original Shape: Oval, in order to accommodate a running track

First match: Stoke City 1–0 Talke Rangers Attendance 2,500

24 September 1883: First game where stadium was named the Victoria Ground, vs. Great Lever

8 September 1888: First Football League game at the Vic, vs. WBA (2–0 to WBA) in front of 4,500 fans

1919: New 2,000-seater stand built at an otherwise open ground

1920s: 2,000-seat stand rebuilt and wooden stand introduced opposite

1930: Boothen End Terrace constructed with roof. The stadium lost its oval shape

1935: Butler Street Stand constructed, covered, 5,000 seats

1939–45: Butler Street stand handed over by club to the British Army as training facility

1956: Floodlights used for first time, vs. Port Vale

1956/57: Floodlit friendlies played to celebrate newly lit stadium vs. Radnicki of Yugoslavia (3–0 to Stoke) and vs. Essen of West Germany (5–0 to Stoke)

1963: Main stand rebuilt again

1970s: Butler Street Stand partly rebuilt following damaging gale, severely affecting club finances

Late 1970s: Two-tiered Stoke End was opened and
    replaced huge open terrace
Last match: 4 May 1997; Stoke City 2–1 West
    Bromwich Albion
Capacity: 22,500
Record Attendance: 51,380, Stoke City vs. Arsenal
    (Div 1), 29 March 1937
Trivia: Floodlights behind the main terrace were
    constructed behind the terrace itself rather than in
    the usual position of in the corners of the pitch

Britannia Stadium
Built on the site of the former Hem Heath Colliery, the
arena became Stoke's home in 1997, after the completion
of the £14.7 million construction of the ground. After its
first season of staging Stoke's home games, the club were
duly relegated, with Manchester City confirming both
the Potters and their own demise with a 5–2 victory on
the final day of the 1997/98 campaign.

The capacity of the Britannia is 28,400, but has
been reduced because of enforced segregation of fans
since their promotion to the Premier League. Stanley
Matthews' ashes are buried under the centre circle of
the pitch upon his request. As well as Stoke matches, the
stadium has also played host to the Conference National
play-off final for three seasons between 2002 and 2004.
On top of this, it has held an England U-21 international
match in 2002, when the youngsters lost 1–0 to their
Portuguese counterparts. Bon Jovi and Bryan Adams
have also performed at City's home ground, though
sadly not as players. . . .

Facts in brief:
Name: Britannia Stadium
Inauguration: 27 August 1997
First match: Stoke City 1–1 Rochdale on 27 August
    1997 in the Worthington Cup in front of 15,439 fans

First Goal: Graham Kavanagh for Stoke in the game
against Rochdale on 27 August 1997

30 August 1997: First ever League game, vs.
Swindon Town in front of 23,859 fans –
City lost 2–1

2007: Club obtains full ownership of the stadium in a
£6m deal

Capacity: 28,383 seats

Record Attendance: 28,218, Stoke City vs. Everton,
5 January 2002

Address: Stanley Matthews Way, Stoke-on-Trent, ST4 4EG

Cost: £15m – built in order to bring the club into
accordance with the Taylor Report

Sponsored by the Britannia Building Society
(£1m per year for ten years)

Football Trust sponsored £3m as a grant in order to
fund building of stadium

L-shaped Boothen and East stands on north and
east sides of stadium hold 6,006 and 8,789 fans
respectively

West Stand holds 7,357 fans as well as media,
banqueting facilities including Tony Waddington
Suite in a two-tier construction

South Stand holds 4,996 away fans and can allow for
segregation that would permit some home fans to use
part of the stand

Club offices, dressing rooms, boardroom and club
superstore are within the south-west corner of the
stadium

Played host to Bon Jovi, Bryan Adams and Busted as a
music concert venue

The stadium is qualified in all aspects, apart from
capacity (which must be 30,000+), to be a UEFA
4-star stadium

The Boothen End is regarded as the most passionate
stand in the stadium, and is compared to that of
Liverpool's Kop

If Stoke establish themselves as a Premier League force,
   plans have been drawn up to expand the stadium
   to over 30,000 by filling in the gap between the
   Boothen End and the West Stand, thus preventing
   the fierce Siberian breeze that often welcomes visiting
   teams!
In between the Seddon End and the South Stand there is
   a large screen

THE PIONEERS

Eleven post-war Stoke City players have quit the
English game to either extend their career or take on a
new challenge in North America. The mid-1970s were
the boom years in the States, with the NASL attracting
players such as Pelé and George Best, but City's first
export had moved to America long before then.

Former Manchester United star Dennis Viollet scored
59 goals in 102 appearances for the Potters during the
1960s but decided to try his luck across the Atlantic by
joining Baltimore Boys in 1967. Terry Lees was next to
quit the Potters for the USA when, after four years at the
Victoria Ground, he moved to San José Earthquakes in
1974.

Eric Skeels appeared more than 500 times in a Stoke
City shirt in a career that spanned 17 years but he ended
his playing days with Seattle Sounders by joining the
West Coast NASL outfit in 1976. He was followed to
Seattle by Jimmy Robertson a year later as the migration
from England became a mini-invasion of footballers
lured by a new way of life and the chance of earning more
money. Former Liverpool full-back Alec Lindsay spent
one season in Stoke-on-Trent before moving to Oakland
Stompers in 1978 and Viv Busby, Ray Evans, Dave
Watson and Paul Maguire all followed the well-trodden

path in the late 1970s and early 1980s before the NASL imploded and collapsed as a commercial concern. The green shoots of recovery in what is now Major League Soccer (MLS) has attracted both Mark Williams (2003) and Paul Williams (2004) in recent years, too.

JOIN THE Q!

If Tony Pulis can sign a player for City with a surname beginning with 'Q', according to my records the Potters will be the only postwar side to have a complete A to Z player database. In other words, they will have had at least one player beginning with each letter of the alphabet. Currently, Stoke have 25 letters of the alphabet with a complete X, Y and Z, but sadly not Q as yet. The unique last three in the list are Davide Xausa who played just one game during the 1997/98 campaign, Tommy Younger who played 10 games between 1959 and 1960 and Fulham's Gaby Zakuani who had two loan spells at the Britannia Stadium between 2006 and 2008. Come on, Pulis – complete the list!

PULIS SAID IT ...

'It is unusual for Stoke over the years to be playing against Manchester United, Liverpool, Chelsea and all the other top clubs. It shows where the club is going, how far we have moved and where we eventually want to go. The next two or three years are probably the most important this club has ever had.'

Pulis gazes into his crystal ball. ...

'Nothing has been decided and nothing is a foregone conclusion. I'll take stock of the situation once we know who we have and haven't signed over the summer. You can't really make a decision before then.'

Pondering the 2009/10 captaincy

'I've been in the game since I was 16 and nothing surprises me any more. I'm obviously disappointed but the chairman has decided to go in a different way and I hope he's made the right decision.'

After leaving the Britannia in 2005

'The most important thing is the club and that it pushes on to get things sorted out before the start of the season. I took the club over and honestly believed that with the right backing we could get into the Premiership.'

He was proved right – just three years later!

'We need to get more goals, but there is no way I will ever move away from having my teams organised, well set and committed. A balance has to be struck. If we can get wide players and forwards who can score, that's what I hope to achieve.

Pulis reveals his blueprint for success

'The fact is, we were top of the league in September 2004 and I was told by the owners I would have £2m to spend to take the club on. We had good players lined up, but, instead, we sold players and I never saw any of the money that was promised to me.'

**Explaining why things didn't work out at City
first time around**

FA YOUTH CUP

The competition that has showcased the emerging talent of players like George Best, Paul Gascoigne, David Beckham and Wayne Rooney was started way back in 1952. After the Second World War, the FA wanted to organise a youth championship for players who had left school but were too young for senior football. Though the championships served a purpose by giving youngsters a bigger platform to show their ability, it was decided that a competition for club sides who were direct members of the FA – regardless of whether they professional or amateur – was the best way forward.

Though crowds were sparse and not every club had a youth team, the competition proved to be popular and quickly became the major event of youth football.

The Potters, by and large, have been mostly disappointing in the competition, reaching the final on just one occasion, during the 1983/84 campaign. City were unfortunate to come up against one of the most successful youth teams in England, Everton, who were the previous season's runners-up. The first leg was played at the Victoria Ground and ended 2–2, but the young Toffees won the second leg 2–0 at Goodison Park to lift the trophy. As the competition enters its 58th year, Stoke fans are still waiting to see their youngsters win the trophy.

FIXED PENALTY

In 1981 the Potters and Manchester City took part in what was, at the time, the longest penalty shoot-out in the history of English football. The first leg of the second-round League Cup tie ended with a 2–0 win for the Blues at Maine Road, while Stoke won the return by the same score. Extra time failed to separate the teams and a penalty shoot-out was the only way of settling the tie. Both sides had top keepers in Peter Fox and Joe Corrigan, but only Fox managed to save one with Lee Chapman missing his effort as the drama unfolded. With the score at 8–8, the visitors converted their ninth successful penalty, Peter Griffiths stepped up and bearing in mind he was the tenth taker out of a possible eleven (Fox was the other), it's easy to guess why his shot was saved by Corrigan!

PLAYER FOCUS:
FACTS, TRIVIA AND STATS ON SOME OF CITY'S GREATEST PLAYERS

Sir Stanley Matthews, CBE
Born: 1 February 1915, Hanley, Stoke-on-Trent
Died: 23 February 2000 (aged 85), Stoke-on-Trent
Position: Outside right
Appearances for Stoke: 318
Goals for Stoke: 54
England Caps: 54
England Goals: 11

- Signed professional contract for Stoke City in 1932
- International debut for England in 1934 vs. Wales in 4–0 win
- Asked for transfer in 1938 which led to protests of up to 3,000 people, causing him to stay
- Stationed near Blackpool during the Second World War with the RAF
- 10 May 1947: Sold to Blackpool for £11,500 at age of 32
- First winner of the Football Writers' Association Footballer of the Year award in 1948

- Won FA Cup Final in 1953 and the game was later dubbed the 'Matthews Final' despite the hat-trick scored by team-mate Stan Mortensen
- 1956: First winner of European Footballer of the Year
- 1957: Awarded CBE in New Year's Honours list
- 15 May 1957: Made final appearance for England 23 years after his debut, which makes him the oldest player to ever play for England
- 1961: Rejoined Stoke City
- 1962/63: Stoke win English Second Division Championship and Matthews is named Football Writers' Association Footballer of the Year for a second time
- 6 February 1965: Appeared in his final match for Stoke and it was claimed even then that he had retired too early
- Played in England's top level until the age of 50 (oldest player ever in England' top flight)
- April 1965: Testimonial match played in honour of Matthews at Victoria Ground where 35,000 people watched a game against a World XI side that included Alfredo Stefano
- 1965: Only player to have been knighted during his playing career
- Matthews never received a booking in 701 games
- July 1965: Appointed General Manager at Port Vale, Stoke City's rivals
- May 1967: Handed complete managerial control
- 1968: Stood down as manager following expulsion from the football league owing to financial irregularities
- 1970/71: Became player/coach at Maltese side Hibernians
- Later served as President of Stoke City following playing spells for various local sides which left him playing into his sixties

- 1992: Awarded FIFA Gold Merit Order
- Following his death in 2000, his ashes were buried underneath the centre spot at Stoke City home ground, the Britannia Stadium
- 2002: Became an inaugural inductee into the English Football Hall of Fame

Sir Geoff Hurst, MBE
Born: 8 December 1941, Ashton-under-Lyne
Position: Striker
Appearances for Stoke: 100
Goals for Stoke: 30
England caps: 49
Goals: 24

- 1959: Signed up by West Ham United and converted from midfielder to striker by then manager Ron Greenwood
- 1964: Won FA Cup, scoring in the final
- 1965: Won UEFA Cup Winners' Cup
- February 1966: Made England debut
- Summer 1966: Brought into first eleven of World Cup squad as Jimmy Greaves suffers gash to leg. Scores in quarter-final, sets up a goal in the semi-final, and becomes the only player to score a hat-trick in a World Cup final in only his eighth international appearance
- 1968: Manchester United have bid of £200,000 rejected
- 1972: West Ham played Stoke City in the semi-finals of the League Cup. Stoke won the round and then the competition
- 1972: Signed by Stoke for £75,000 as the club sought to address the possible retirement of John Ritchie
- 1975: Left Stoke for WBA in order to wind down career

- 1975: Awarded the MBE
- 1976: Moved to Seattle Sounders scoring 9 goals in 24 appearances
- 1977–82: Assistant manager of national squad under Ron Greenwood
- 1979–81: Manager of Chelsea
- 1998: Knighted
- 2004: Inducted into English Football Hall of Fame

Gordon Banks, OBE
Born: 30 December 1937, Sheffield
Position: Goalkeeper
Appearances for Stoke: 246
England Caps: 73

- 1955: Signed as an apprentice by Chesterfield
- November 1958: Senior debut for Chesterfield against Colchester United in newly formed Third Division
- 1959: Signed by Leicester City for £7,000
- April 1963: England debut vs. Scotland
- 1964: Beat Stoke City 4–3 over two legs to win League Cup
- 1966: Kept four clean sheets in the first four games of the World Cup and went on to win the tournament
- 1966: Found himself available for transfer once Peter Shilton demanded first team football and signed for Stoke City for £52,000
- 1967: Played a season for Cleveland Stokers in the USA, as the country attempted to build a soccer league by importing foreign sides
- 1969: Won 50th cap, vs. Scotland
- 1970: Made the 'Pelé' save in the World Cup group game with Brazil
- 1970: Became Stoke's most capped player at senior international level

- 1970: Awarded OBE
- 1972: Won League Cup, named Footballer of the Year and named Sportsman of the Year
- 22 October 1972: Involved in an incident on the road that caused him to lose the sight in his right eye, ending his Stoke City career
- 1977/78: Played for US side Fort Lauderdale Strikers as a World Football Superstar against former rival George Best
- Elected by the International Federation of Football History & Statistics as the second best goalkeeper of the twentieth century, behind Lev Yashin and ahead of Dino Zoff

Peter Shilton, OBE
Born: 18 September 1949, Leicester
Position: Goalkeeper
Appearances for Stoke: 120
England caps: 125

- 1963: Signed as a schoolboy by Leicester City
- May 1966: Makes professional debut vs. Everton
- 1966: Shilton demanded the promise of first-team football if he was to sign a new contract and so Leicester transfer-listed Gordon Banks
- October 1967: Scores goal against Southampton direct from a clearance
- 1969: Relegated but also FA Cup runner-up
- November 1970: Makes England debut vs. East Germany
- 1971: Promoted back to first division
- 1972: England number one Gordon Banks loses the sight in one eye and left England's selectors to choose between Peter Shilton and Ray Clemence as England number one
- 1974: Signed for Stoke City for £325,000 needing a new challenge

- 1975: Ray Clemence became the favoured England goalkeeper as Don Revie handed him eight out of nine possible starts. Shilton played once for England in 1975, not at all in 1976 and only twice in 1977
- 1976: Shilton pulls out of bicentennial celebration tournament in the US and asked not to be considered again, changing his mind three months later.
- 1976: Stoke agree fee of £275,000 for Shilton, offered by Manchester United but United refused to pay Shilton the wages he was demanding
- 1977: As Stoke were relegated, Shilton asked for a transfer, eventually moving to Nottingham Forest for £250,000
- 1977/78: Shilton concedes only 18 goals in 37 appearances, leading to him winning the PFA Player of the Year Award
- 1979: Wins League Cup and European Cup
- 1979: Wins European Super Cup
- 1980: Wins second European Cup. Ron Greenwood acknowledged Shilton's return to form by beginning to alternate between Shilton and Clemence, something his club manager Brian Clough was offended by
- 1982: Shilton joins Southampton
- 1986: Conceded the infamous 'Hand of God' goal
- 1987: Shilton leaves The Dell for Derby County
- June 1989: Shilton becomes England's most capped player ahead of Bobby Moore, gaining his 109th cap vs. Denmark
- 1990: Awarded the Order of Merit by the PFA
- 1991: Awarded Football Writers' Tribute Award
- 1989/90: Conceded no goals whatsoever in qualifying for the 1990 World Cup
- 1991: Rejected offer to become manager of Hull City
- 1992: Became player-manager of Plymouth Argyle

- 22 December 1996: Played his 1,000th game, in a match between Leyton Orient and Brighton & Hove Albion
- 2002: Made an inaugural inductee of the English Football Hall of Fame
- Holds record for the most appearances in world football

Alan Hudson
Born: 21 June 1951, Chelsea
Position: Midfielder
Games: 144
Goals: 9
England caps: 2
Goals: 0

- 1 February 1969: Senior debut for Chelsea against Southampton nine months after injury had stopped him becoming Chelsea's youngest ever player
- 1970: He played every game of Chelsea's 1970 FA Cup run except the victorious final vs. Leeds United because of injury
- 1971: Played a major role in Chelsea's replayed European Cup Winners' Cup final
- January 1974: Placed on the Chelsea transfer list following a fall-out with Chelsea manager Dave Sexton and signed by Stoke City for a fee of £240,000 at the age of 22 in February 1974
- 1975: Made England debut following a ban from international football, having refused to play for the England Under-23 side, while injury and arguments with then England manager Don Revie ensured that caps against West Germany and Cyprus were the only ones that he earned

- December 1976: Sold to Arsenal for a fee of £200,000 due to Stoke City's poor financial position – a team that he helped to reach the 1978 FA Cup final which they went on to lose 1–0 to Ipswich Town
- 1978: Moved to Seattle Sounders for a fee of £100,000 because of differences between him and his manager and went on to play for Cleveland Force and Hércules CF in Spain before returning to Chelsea
- 1984: Returned to Stoke City where he helped them avoid relegation
- After retirement, Hudson was affected by alcoholism and bankruptcy as well as being in a coma between December 1997 and February 1998 following a car accident
- Hudson released autobiography *The Working Man's Ballet* which led to him being offered a post with the *Stoke Evening Sentinel* and the *Sporting Life* and in 2008 Hudson released a book entitled *The Waddington Years*, which told of his great relationship with the former Stoke manager
- 2004: Appeared in *The Football Factory* in a cameo role

John Ritchie

Born: 12 July 1941, Kettering
Died: 23 February 2007 (aged 65)
Position: Striker
Appearances for Stoke: 343
Goals for Stoke: 176 (club's top scorer)

- June 1962: Signed by Stoke City for £2,500 from Kettering Town, reportedly without the manager seeing him play, merely based on the recommendation of a scout
- April 1963: Makes Stoke debut
- May 1963: Stoke win Second Division Championship

- 1966: Sold to Sheffield Wednesday for £70,000
- 1969: Re-signed by Stoke for £25,000 and Stoke manager Toy Waddington admits that he should never have sold him
- 1971: FA Cup Finalist
- 1972: Sent off for punching an opponent in a UEFA Cup game after 29 seconds of the game without even touching the ball
- 1972: FA Cup Finalist
- 1972: Stoke win League Cup
- Acquired the nickname of 'Reggie' while at Stoke yet no-one understood why
- March 1974: Criticised by Peter Osgood as only capable of scoring by means of aerial prowess. In response, when Stoke next played Osgood's Southampton, Ritchie stooped down, knelt to the ground and nudged the ball over the line of the unoccupied goal with his head. He completed a hat-trick that day
- 1975: Stoke career ended by double leg fracture
- A brief spell at non-league Stafford Rangers followed

Freddie Steele
Born: 6 May 1916, Hanley, Stoke-on-Trent
Died: 23 April 1976 (aged 59), Newcastle-under-Lyme
Position: Forward
Appearances for Stoke: 346
Goals for Stoke: 220 (including wartime)
England caps: 6
Goals: 8

- 1931: Signed for Stoke at the age of 15 and worked in the club offices until he was old enough to play for the club professionally
- August 1933: Signed first professional contract for club

- Nicknamed 'Nobby' by fans
- 17 October 1936: Makes England debut vs. Wales
- 4 February 1937: Scored 5 goals in Stoke's record win of 10–3 over WBA
- 1936/37: Scored a record number of goals in a season for Stoke (33)
- 1937: Knee injury sidelined him all season
- 1939: Steele retired from football aged 23 only to return and score 10 goals in his first 5 games. Returned to the club in 1945 (after the war) scoring 49 goals in 43 games on his return
- 1949: Persistent injury caused him to leave the club and he was appointed player-manager of Mansfield Town
- 1951: Appointed player-manager of Stoke City's rivals Port Vale
- December 1952: Dropped himself as a player in order to focus on management
- 1962: Returned to Port Vale to manage the club until 1965

Eric Skeels
Born: 27 October 1939, Eccles
Position: Defender
Appearances for Stoke: 575
Goals for Stoke: 7

- Supposedly wrote to Stoke requesting a trial while playing for Stockport County aged 19
- 1959: Made Stoke City debut
- Nicknamed 'Mr Dependable'
- 1963: Won Second Division title
- 1964: League Cup runners-up
- Player to have made the most appearances for Stoke City
- 1976: Left Stoke at the age of 36 to sign for Seattle Sounders

- 1976: After short spell in the US, Skeels signed for Stoke City's rivals Port Vale
- May 1977: Handed free transfer to Leek Town

Mark Stein
Full Name: Earl Mark Sean Stein
Born: 29 January 1966, Cape Town
Position: Striker

- 1984/85: Made his professional debut for Luton Town
- 1988: Winner of League Cup final with Luton Town after shock 3–2 win over Arsenal in the final. It remains Luton's only major honour in their history
- 1991: Loaned out and eventually bought by Stoke City, becoming a huge fan favourite with various goals over local rivals Port Vale
- 1993: Sold to Chelsea for £1.5m
- December 2003–February 1994: Set a record of scoring in seven consecutive matches, a record that stood until 2002 when Ruud van Nistlerooy surpassed it
- 1994: Appeared in FA Cup final
- 1996: Loaned back to Stoke City in a move that was not made permanent
- 12 July 2008: Played in Gordon Banks charity match at the Britannia Stadium for the England XI
- Currently a physio with Barnet FC
- Younger brother of former Luton Town striker Brian Stein

Alan Bloor
Born: 16 March 1943, Stoke-on-Trent
Position: Centre-half

- 1960: Signed for Stoke City as a schoolboy aged 17
- 1961: Made professional debut for Stoke City

- 1972: Winner of League Cup
- 1973: Winner of the Watney Cup
- Praised by Sir Matt Busby
- Made more than 370 appearances for Stoke City
- June 1978: Moved to Port Vale as a player and youth team coach
- September 1978: After only six league appearances, retired from the playing side of the game and focused on coaching role
- August 1979: Appointed Port Vale caretaker manager to later be handed the full-time post in September 1979
- December 1979: Resigned from management role claiming that he was not up to the job

Frank Soo

Born: 12 March 1914, Buxton
Died: 25 January 1991 (aged 76), Cheadle
Position: Inside Forward
Appearances for Stoke: 266
Goals for Stoke: 34 (including wartime)
England caps: 9 Goals: 0

- Began career with Prescot Cables as a youth team player
- January 1933: Signed for Stoke City and became first player of Chinese origin to play in the football league
- November 1933: Stoke City debut vs. Middlesbrough
- 9 May 1942: Became first non-white player to play for England
- Guested for Chelsea, Millwall and Everton during the war
- September 1945: Signed for Leicester for £4,600 rejoining Tom Mather who signed him for Stoke
- July 1946: Signed for Luton Town for £5,000

- 1948: Signed for Chelmsford for £2,500 and became a free-kick specialist
- April 1950: Appointed manager of Padova and remained there until 1952
- Also managed Orebro, Djurgardens, AIK and St Alban's City as well as the Israeli national side

Neil Franklin

Born: 24 Jaunary 1922, Shelton
Died: 9 February 1996 (aged 74), Stoke-on-Trent
Position: Defender
Appearances for Stoke: 162
Goals for Stoke: 0
England caps: 27 Goals: 0

- Starred for Stoke's junior side Stoke Old Boys
- January 1939: Signed as a professional for Stoke City
- Progress of career stunted by start of the war but he represented Stoke and England in wartime friendlies
- 1945–50: Established himself as one of the country's best defenders
- 1946: England debut
- 1950: Chose to leave Stoke because he was unhappy about the £20 a week maximum wage limit and 'dirty' air
- Broke contract with Stoke in order to move to Columbian side Independiente Santa Fé of Bogotá
- Franklin caused controversy with this move as the Columbian FA was considered a rebel authority as it was outside of FIFA jurisdiction
- 1950: Franklin rejected the opportunity to join up with the England squad for the 1950 FA Cup finals

- Four weeks after moving to Columbia, social and political issues made it difficult for his family to settle and caused him to move back to England
- The Football League suspended Franklin and he never played for England or Stoke again
- February 1951: Franklin moved to Hull City for £22,500, a world record fee for a defender at the time
- Brief spells at Crewe, Stockport and Mansfield
- 1963: Appointed manager of Colchester United and remained there until 1968

Leigh Richmond Roose
Born: 27 November 1877, Holt, Wales
Died: 7 October 1916 (aged 38), Western Front, France
Position: Goalkeeper
Appearances for Stoke: 147
Wales caps: 24

- 1895: Began footballing career with Aberystwyth
- 1900: Won Welsh Cup final with man-of-the-match performance
- 24 February 1900: Wales debut vs. Ireland
- 1901: Signed by Stoke City as an amateur
- Voted World XI goalkeeper in a *Daily Mail* poll
- 1904/05: Moved to Everton for a one-year spell before returning to Stoke City
- 1905: Re-signed by Stoke and the club saw attendances treble
- 1907: Stoke City contract terminated due to broken wrist
- 5 March 1910: Conceded a goal for Wales against Scotland while he was talking to a spectator and an opponent shot from distance
- December 1911: Signed as player/coach for Arsenal

- 1916: Killed towards the end of the Battle of the Somme
- Famous for tactic in which he would bounce the ball up to the half way line before a long throw or kick up to his strikers
- Also famous for implementing the shaky legs tactic as an opponent prepared to take a penalty

George Eastham, OBE
Born: 23 September 1936, Blackpool
Position: Inside Forward, Midfielder
Appearances for Stoke: 194
Goals for Stoke: 4
England Caps: 19 Goals: 2

- Began football career with Northern Irish side Ards
- 1956: Signed for Newcastle scoring 29 in 124 appearances before choosing to leave due to the unsatisfactory living accommodation he was provided and the club's attempts to stop him playing for the England Under-23 squad
- Newcastle refused him a transfer, he went on strike during the 1959/60 season
- October 1960: Signed for Arsenal for £47,500 scoring 40 goals in 207 appearances
- 18 August 1960: Signed for Stoke City for £35,000
- 1963: Noted as a key member of the case that improved players' freedom to move between clubs
- 1966: Non-playing member of the World Cup winning squad
- February 1971: Eastham sought to secure a position for himself in football after his playing days were over so he spent time in South Africa playing on loan for Cape Town City before taking up a post as player-manager of Hellenic FC
- October 1971: Eastham returned to Stoke to continue playing career

- 1972: Scored winner in the League Cup final vs. Chelsea and became oldest ever winner of the competition
- 1972/73: Played in the UEFA Cup for Stoke
- 1973: Awarded the OBE
- Became Tony Waddington's assistant manager at Stoke
- 1977: Succeeded Waddington as manager
- Relegation from the First Division in 1976/77 season
- January 1978: Eastham left Stoke

Frank Bowyer

Born: 10 April 1922, Chesterton
Died: 1999
Position: Inside Forward
Appearances for Stoke: 436
Goals for Stoke: 149

- June 1937: Joined Stoke City
- 1939: Signed first professional contract for Stoke City
- The outbreak of the Second World War interrupted Bowyer's career so much so that it was not until February 1948 that Bowyer made his football league debut vs. Manchester United
- 1950: Despite never earning a full international cap, Bowyer did represent England in a tour of Canada
- 1953: Relegated from Division One
- 1959/60: Finishes season as Stoke's top scorer at the age of 38
- Finished Stoke career only four league goals behind all time leader Freddie Steele who had 140 to his name
- 1960: Bowyer left Stoke to become player-manager of Macclesfield Town

James Beattie
Born: 27 February 1978, Lancaster
Position: Striker

- Rated the second best swimmer in the country at 100m swimming freestyle as a school boy but chose football over swimming
- 12 October 1996: Made professional debut for Blackburn Rovers vs. Arsenal
- July 1998: Signed for Southampton for £1m as part of deal that took Kevin Davies to Blackburn for £7m
- November 2000: Despite a drought of eighteen months without a goal (mainly due to injury) Beattie went on to score ten goals in ten games but then only scored two goals for the rest of the season which resulted in a run of seventeen games without a goal that spanned over two seasons
- 2002-2003: Highest English goal scorer for the season with 23 league goals in the same season as he helped the Saints to FA Cup Final
- 12 February 2003: England debut vs. Australia, played 45 minutes and was judged to be ineffective, his inconsistent career has meant that he has not appeared for his country since the Euro 2004 qualifiers
- January 2005: Signed for Everton for £6m (Everton's record fee spent) but first season was remembered not for goal scoring but for a head butt on William Gallas that saw Beattie sent off in only fifth appearance for club. However, in 2005/06 Beattie was Everton's top scorer with ten league goals
- 4 August 2007: Signed for Sheffield United for £4m (Sheffield United's record fee spent)

- 2 October 2007: Awarded Coca-Cola Championship player of the month which sparked rumours of a return to the Premier League with Aston Villa and scored 22 goals that season resulting in him being awarded the club's player of the season in May 2008
- 12 January 2009: Signed by Stoke City for a proposed £2.5m deal that was brokered in an attempt to bolster Stoke's attacking options in their battle against relegation – he scored four goals in first five appearances

A POTTED HISTORY OF, ER, THE POTTERS

1863

Apprentices at the North Staffordshire Railway, all former pupils from the prestigious independent boarding school Charterhouse, formed a football club called Stoke Ramblers.

1868

The *Field* magazine confirmed that a new football club had been created in Stoke-on-Trent with its founder listed to be Henry Almond. The newly-formed team's first recorded match was in October 1868 against an E.W. May XV and was played at Victoria Cricket Ground. Almond scored the club's first ever goal (yes, straight in the net off his nut), although he left the club soon after to pursue a career as a civil engineer.

1875

Rising crowds saw the club move to Sweetings Field.

1878
Stoke Football Club merged with Stoke Victoria Cricket Club and moved grounds again – this time to the Athletics Club Ground, soon to be known better as the Victoria Ground.

1888
Stoke were one of the twelve founding members of the Football League, along with Preston North End, Aston Villa, Wolves, Blackburn, Bolton, West Brom, Accrington, Everton, Burnley, Derby and Notts County. The Potters finished bottom in each of their first two seasons.

1908
Stoke had some fine players, but owing to financial trouble, could not hold onto them and the club went temporarily out of business. Having lost their league status in the summer of 1908, the club fielded a side in the Birmingham & District League and another in the Southern League, winning all ten matches and scoring 48 goals.

1915
Stoke were re-elected into the Football League – but then the outbreak of the First World War meant there was no football for several years.

1919
The club bought the Victoria Ground and built the 12,000-seater Butler Street stand, pushing the overall capacity to 50,000.

1925
Stoke-on-Trent won city status and therefore the club officially became Stoke City FC.

1932

The 17-year-old Stanley Matthews joined Stoke as an apprentice and made his debut against Bury in March 1932. He also went on to become the first Stoke player to put on an England shirt for 30 years.

1937

The Potters scored a record League win of 10–3 against West Brom and also posted a record gate of 51,373 in April of the same year during a match with Arsenal. Freddie Steele made it a triple record that season by bagging 33 League goals

1939

The outbreak of the Second World War in 1939 meant City and their star players were somewhat frozen in time. The club ticked along with wartime football and a mixture of amateurs and guest players.

1946

A crush barrier gave way during a game with Bolton and 33 spectators died while a further 520 were injured.

1947

City needed to win their final game of the season to be crowned League champions but a 2–1 defeat at Sheffield United meant Liverpool won the title instead. Stanley Matthews joined Blackpool aged 32.

1952

Tony Waddington joined City as a coach.

1953

Stoke were relegated in 1953 in what was generally a miserable decade for the club. Crowds dipped below 10,000 for the first time since 1919.

1960

Waddington became manager and convinced the 46-year-old Matthews to rejoin the club during his first season in charge. Waddington brought in new tactics that would be known as 'Waddington's Wall' – no, not a family game you bring out of a dusty cupboard at Christmas, but rather a defensive tactic that proved a great success.

1961

Attendances were still low but Matthews' signing attracted 35,974 people to the Victoria Ground to see his homecoming game, with gate receipts wiping out his £3,000 transfer fee in that game alone.

1972

On 4 March, City finally won their first major trophy by beating Chelsea 2–1 at Wembley, securing the League Cup in front of a crowd of 97,852. The club then splashed out a world record of £325,000 transfer fee for goalkeeper Peter Shilton from Leicester City.

1976

The club struggled financially again after a roof was blown off during heavy winds in January. The cost of repairs was £250,000 and led to the sale of several key players – Jimmy Greenhoff, Mike Pejic and Alan Hudson – for a combined fee of £440,000. Their inevitable relegation followed at the end of the 1976/77 campaign and Tony Waddington departed the club.

1977

After 14 seasons in the top division, City were relegated.

1979

The Potters finished third behind Crystal Palace and Brighton to clinch promotion back to the top division.

1984

City's youngsters reached the FA Youth Cup Final, drawing the first leg 2–2 at the Victoria Ground before losing the return 2–0 and the tie 4–2 on aggregate to Everton.

1985

The Potters were relegated to Division Two after six seasons in the top league. The club finished rock-bottom with an appalling points haul of 17 from a possible 126 and a goal difference of -67! Here are the 1984/85 stats just for good measure, and please, don't have nightmares:

Pld	W	D	L	F	A	W	D	L	F	A	Pts
42	3	3	15	18	41	0	5	16	6	50	17

1990

The Potters were relegated to Division Three after finishing bottom of the League with the following record:

Pld	W	D	L	F	A	W	D	L	F	A	Pts
46	4	11	8	20	24	2	8	13	15	39	37

1992

Under Lou Macari, City won the Autoglass Trophy.

1993

City were crowned Division Two champions with the following league record:

Pld	W	D	L	F	A	W	D	L	F	A	Pts
46	17	4	2	41	13	10	8	5	32	21	93

1998

City were relegated back to Division Three after 5–2 home defeat to Manchester City.

2000
City won the Auto Windscreens Shield at Wembley and the trophy cabinet threatens to buckle under the strain!

2002
The Potters beat Brentford 2–0 in the Division Two play-off final at the Millennium Stadium.

2008
Manager Tony Pulis guided City to the Premier League for the first time, and the club comfortably survived its first season among the mega-rich, finishing in twelfth place – a fantastic achievement.

2011
The Potters' epic FA Cup run comes to an end with a 1–0 defeat to Manchester City in the 2010/11 final at Wembley. Yaya Touré's winner proves enough to end Stoke's resistance. However, the Potters are back in Europe and reach the last 32 of the Europa League after progressing from the group stages.

WARTIME FOOTBALL – LEAGUE RECORDS

First World War

1915/16

P 36	W 14	D 7	L 15	F 64	A 64

1916/17

P 36	W 19	D 7	L 10	F 75	A 42

1917/18

P 38	W 25	D 6	L 7	F 120	A 34

1918/19

P 36	W 22	D 5	L 9	F 93	A 46

*Second World War**
1939/40

P 30   W 18   D 6   L 6   F 78   A 49

1940/41

P 38   W 10   D 9   L 19   F 39   A 102

1941/42

P 38   W 21   D 4   L 13   F 116   A 85

1942/43

P 38   W 21   D 7   L 10   F 88   A 59

1943/44

P 39   W 16   D 8   L 15   F 106   A 80

1944/45

P 41   W 21   D 6   L 14   F 104   A 65

1945/46

P 50   W 20   D 8   A 22   F 98   A 92

Total

P 420   W 207   D 73   L 140   F 951   A 718

* Figures include the FA Cup ties of 1945/46, the friendlies of 1939/40 & 1940/41 and the three void league games of 1939/40.

MISCELLANEOUS TROPHIES

Birmingham League Cup
1909/10
1st Round – 20 September – Brierley Hill All (h) 2–2
1st Round Replay – 18 October – Brierley Hill All (a) 5–0
2nd Round – 1 November – Stourbridge (h) 3–1
3rd Round – 9 April – Aston Villa (a) 1–2

RICARDO FULLER:
QUOTES BY HIM AND ABOUT HIM

'He's been fantastic for Stoke, he's a breath of fresh air and his goals have helped them stay in the Premier League.'

Former Jamaica boss John Barnes (2009)

'It was the first time in the Premier League for 25 years for the club and we managed to stay up, so this was a tremendous and very satisfying feeling, especially when you know that you helped put back the pride on a lot of people's faces.'

A proud Ricardo reflects on a job well done (2009)

'When you're among the best players in the world you have to try and aim to be the best, because, without trying to be the best, you're going to be nobody.'

Poignant words from RF

'We've got a good group of players who care about things and Ricardo Fuller cared too much – we'll deal with it in house, not through the media.'

Tony Pulis on the Fuller/Griffin spat v West Ham (2008)

'I just said to Griff, "clear the ball out," and he was just very rude and disrespectful so that's what happened. It's all done and dusted now. What he said was bad but what I did was worse. And I'm going to be suspended now for three or four games. So I'm looking forward to the new year now, hopefully it will be a better one for me.'

Ricardo explains his controversial Andy Griffin slap (2008)

'There is never smoke without fire really, but it happened and that's all. I feel sorry for the fans, especially, and for costing the team three points. Hopefully it doesn't happen again.'

More Fuller thoughts on the Griff incident

'They make it so much easier for me to score goals. I have Liam Lawrence and Glenn Whelan feeding me with balls all the time, while Matty Etherington does the same from on the left. Then there is Rory Delap who throws the ball straight onto my head, and of course not forgetting James Beattie who does all of my running for me.'

Ricardo reveals he actually doesn't do anything, while modestly collecting his Goal of the Season award!

NOTABLE TRANSFER LANDMARKS

The first six-figure transfer fee City paid was in 1969 to acquire the services of Birmingham city striker Jimmy Greenhoff. That record lasted four years until it was smashed by the £240,000 signing of Alan Hudson from Chelsea. Ten months later and the Potters set another club record – and a record fee for a goalkeeper in England – when Peter Shilton followed in Gordon Banks' footsteps by leaving Leicester City for the Victoria Ground at a cost of £325,000.

It would be eight years before the record was broken again – this time City paid Manchester United £350,000 for attacking midfielder Sammy McIlroy. Another gap of seven years followed before Ian Cranson was purchased from Sheffield Wednesday for £450,000, but it was a measure of the club's finances that an entire decade passed before that fee was surpassed. In December 1999, City paid Orgryte £600,000 for Brynjar Gunnarsson. Samebegou Bangoura's fee in August 2005 was believed to top the Gunnarsson deal but it was undisclosed for some reason and the first £1 million Stoke City player was Ryan Shawcross, who signed from Manchester United in January 2008. That record lasted a matter of days as Tony Pulis opened his war-chest in a bid to secure promotion to the top flight. £1.2 million was the price Crystal Palace demanded for Leon Cort during the 2008 January transfer window, but even that only lasted seven months before the record was well and truly demolished by the £5.5 million payment to Reading for striker Dave Kitson. That was eclipsed by the £10m bringing England international Peter Crouch to the Britannia from Tottenham Hotspur.

STOKE CITY FC ROLL OF HONOUR

League Cup Winners: 1971/72
Division Two Champions: 1932/33, 1962/63, 1992/93
Division Three (North) Champions: 1926/27
Division Two Play-Off Winners: 2001/02
Auto Windscreens Shield Winners: 1999/2000
Autoglass Trophy Winners: 1991/92
Watney Cup Winners: 1973/74
Football Alliance League Champions: 1890/91
Birmingham & District League Champions: 1910/11
Southern League Division Two Champions: 1914/15
Staffordshire Senior Cup Winners: 1877/78, 1878/79,
    1903/04 (shared), 1913/14, 1964/65, 1968/69
    (shared), 1970/71, 1974/75, 1975/76, 1981/82,
    1992/93, 1994/95, 1998/99
Birmingham Senior Cup Winners: 1900/01, 1913/14
War League Western Division Champions: 1939/40
Isle of Man Trophy Winners: 1987/88, 1991/92,
    1992/93
Bass Charity Vase Winners: 1997/98
UEFA Cup 1st Round: 1972/73, 1974/75

Coca-Cola Championship Runners-Up: 2007/08
League Cup Runners-Up: 1963/64
Division Two Runners-Up: 1921/22
Division Two 3rd Place (Promoted): 1978/79
Southern League Division Two Runners-Up: 1910/11
Staffordshire Senior Cup Runners-Up: 1882/83,
    1885/86, 1895/96, 1900/01, 1901/02, 1902/03,
    2002/03, 2005/06
Birmingham Senior Cup Runners-Up: 1909/10,
    1914/15, 1919/20, 1920/21
Isle of Man Trophy Runners-Up: 1985/86
FA Youth Cup Runners-Up: 1983/84
BBC Midlands Sports Awards Team of the Year: 1992,
    1993, 2008
WKD Nuts Team of the Season: 2008/09

DEANO SAID IT...

Words of wisdom from City's £3m signing Dean
Whitehead

'The lads have got a great spirit here at Stoke and
hopefully I can fit into that. I spoke to Liam Lawrence
and Danny Higginbotham a couple of times, and it
obviously helps knowing people here.'

DW – feeling at home already

'I spoke to Tony Pulis a couple of times as well and he
was a big influence. He's got big plans for this place,
hopefully we'll be progressing and hopefully I can be a
part of that.'

Deano getting with the project

'I'm delighted to be here. I've known of the club's interest
for about six months or so now so it has gone on for a
while.'

Dean Whitehead, clearly pleased to join the Potters

CITY'S COMPLETE LEAGUE RECORD

		HOME					AWAY					
Pld	W	D	L	F	A	W	D	L	F	A	Pts	Pos
2011/12 Premier League												
38	7	8	4	25	20	4	4	11	11	33	46	14th
2010/11 Premier League												
38	10	4	5	31	18	3	3	13	15	30	46	13th
2009/10 Premier League												
38	7	6	6	24	21	4	8	7	10	27	47	11th
2008/09 Premier League												
38	10	5	4	22	15	2	4	13	16	40	45	12th
2007/08 Championship												
46	12	7	4	36	27	9	9	5	33	28	79	2nd
2006/07 Championship												
46	12	8	3	35	16	7	8	8	27	25	73	8th
2005/06 Championship												
46	7	5	11	24	32	10	2	11	30	31	58	13th
2004/05 Championship												
46	11	2	10	22	18	6	8	9	14	20	61	12th
2003/04 Division One												
46	11	7	5	35	24	7	5	11	23	31	66	11th
2002/03 Division One												
46	9	6	8	25	25	3	8	12	20	44	50	21st
2001/02 Division Two												
46	16	4	3	43	12	7	7	9	24	28	80	5th
2000/01 Division Two												
46	12	6	5	39	21	9	8	6	35	28	77	5th
1999/2000 Division Two												
46	13	7	3	37	18	10	6	7	31	24	82	6th
1998/99 Division Two												
46	10	4	9	32	32	11	2	10	27	31	69	8th

| | HOME | | | | | AWAY | | | | | | |
Pld	W	D	L	F	A	W	D	L	F	A	Pts	Pos

1997/98 Division One

| 46 | 8 | 5 | 10 | 30 | 40 | 3 | 8 | 12 | 14 | 34 | 47 | 23rd |

1996/97 Division One

| 46 | 15 | 3 | 5 | 34 | 22 | 3 | 7 | 13 | 17 | 35 | 64 | 12th |

1995/96 Division One

| 46 | 13 | 6 | 4 | 32 | 15 | 7 | 7 | 9 | 28 | 34 | 73 | 4th |

1994/95 Division One

| 46 | 10 | 7 | 6 | 31 | 21 | 6 | 8 | 9 | 19 | 32 | 63 | 11th |

1993/94 Division One

| 46 | 14 | 4 | 5 | 35 | 19 | 4 | 9 | 10 | 22 | 40 | 67 | 10th |

1992/93 Division Two

| 46 | 17 | 4 | 2 | 41 | 13 | 10 | 8 | 5 | 32 | 21 | 93 | 1st |

1991/92 Third Division

| 46 | 14 | 5 | 4 | 45 | 24 | 7 | 9 | 7 | 24 | 25 | 77 | 4th |

1990/91 Third Division

| 46 | 9 | 7 | 7 | 36 | 29 | 7 | 5 | 11 | 19 | 30 | 60 | 14th |

1989/90 Second Division

| 46 | 4 | 11 | 8 | 20 | 24 | 2 | 8 | 13 | 15 | 39 | 37 | 24th |

1988/89 Second Division

| 46 | 10 | 9 | 4 | 33 | 25 | 5 | 5 | 13 | 24 | 47 | 59 | 13th |

1987/88 Second Division

| 44 | 12 | 6 | 4 | 34 | 22 | 5 | 5 | 12 | 16 | 35 | 62 | 11th |

1986/87 Second Division

| 42 | 11 | 5 | 5 | 40 | 21 | 5 | 5 | 11 | 23 | 32 | 58 | 8th |

1985/86 Second Division

| 42 | 8 | 11 | 2 | 29 | 16 | 6 | 4 | 11 | 19 | 34 | 57 | 10th |

1984/85 First Division

| 42 | 3 | 3 | 15 | 18 | 41 | 0 | 5 | 16 | 6 | 50 | 17 | 22nd |

1983/84 First Division

| 42 | 11 | 4 | 6 | 30 | 23 | 2 | 7 | 12 | 14 | 40 | 50 | 18th |

	HOME					AWAY						
Pld	W	D	L	F	A	W	D	L	F	A	Pts	Pos
1982/83 First Division												
42	13	4	4	34	21	3	5	13	19	43	57	13th
1981/82 First Division												
42	9	2	10	27	28	3	6	12	17	35	44	18th
1980/81 First Division												
42	8	9	4	31	23	4	9	8	20	37	42	11th
1979/80 First Division												
42	9	4	8	27	26	4	6	11	17	32	36	18th
1978/79 Second Division												
42	11	7	3	35	15	9	9	3	23	16	56	3rd
1977/78 Second Division												
42	13	5	3	38	16	3	5	13	15	33	42	7th
1976/77 First Division												
42	9	8	4	21	16	1	6	14	7	5	34	21st
1975/76 First Division												
42	8	5	8	25	24	7	6	8	23	26	41	12th
1974/75 First Division												
42	12	7	2	40	18	5	8	8	24	30	49	5th
1973/74 First Division												
42	13	6	2	39	15	2	10	9	15	27	46	5th
1972/73 First Division												
42	11	8	2	38	17	3	2	16	23	39	38	15th
1971/72 First Division												
42	6	10	5	26	25	4	5	12	13	31	35	17th
1970/71 First Division												
42	10	7	4	28	11	2	6	13	16	37	37	13th
1969/70 First Division												
42	10	7	4	31	23	5	8	8	25	29	45	9th
1968/69 First Division												
42	9	7	5	24	24	0	8	13	16	39	33	19th

	HOME					AWAY					
Pld	W	D	L	F	A	W	D	L	F	A	Pts	Pos

1967/68 First Division

| 42 | 10 | 3 | 8 | 30 | 29 | 4 | 4 | 13 | 20 | 44 | 35 | 18th |

1966/67 First Division

| 42 | 11 | 5 | 5 | 40 | 21 | 6 | 2 | 13 | 23 | 37 | 41 | 12th |

1965/66 First Division

| 42 | 12 | 6 | 3 | 42 | 22 | 3 | 6 | 12 | 23 | 42 | 42 | 10th |

1964/65 First Division

| 42 | 11 | 4 | 6 | 40 | 27 | 5 | 6 | 10 | 27 | 39 | 42 | 11th |

1963/64 First Division

| 42 | 9 | 6 | 6 | 49 | 33 | 5 | 4 | 12 | 28 | 45 | 38 | 17th |

1962/63 Second Division

| 42 | 15 | 3 | 3 | 49 | 20 | 5 | 10 | 6 | 24 | 30 | 53 | 1st |

1961/62 Second Division

| 42 | 13 | 4 | 4 | 34 | 17 | 4 | 4 | 13 | 21 | 40 | 42 | 8th |

1960/61 Second Division

| 42 | 9 | 6 | 6 | 39 | 26 | 3 | 6 | 12 | 12 | 33 | 36 | 18th |

1959/60 Second Division

| 42 | 8 | 3 | 10 | 40 | 38 | 6 | 4 | 11 | 26 | 45 | 35 | 17th |

1958/59 Second Division

| 42 | 16 | 2 | 3 | 48 | 19 | 5 | 5 | 11 | 24 | 39 | 49 | 5th |

1957/58 Second Division

| 42 | 9 | 4 | 8 | 49 | 36 | 9 | 2 | 10 | 26 | 37 | 42 | 11th |

1956/57 Second Division

| 42 | 16 | 2 | 3 | 64 | 18 | 4 | 6 | 11 | 19 | 40 | 48 | 5th |

1955/56 Second Division

| 42 | 13 | 2 | 6 | 47 | 27 | 7 | 2 | 12 | 24 | 35 | 44 | 13th |

1954/55 Second Division

| 42 | 12 | 5 | 4 | 38 | 17 | 9 | 5 | 7 | 31 | 29 | 52 | 5th |

1953/54 Second Division

| 42 | 8 | 8 | 5 | 43 | 28 | 4 | 9 | 8 | 28 | 32 | 41 | 11th |

	HOME					AWAY						
Pld	W	D	L	F	A	W	D	L	F	A	Pts	Pos

1952/53 First Division

Pld	W	D	L	F	A	W	D	L	F	A	Pts	Pos
42	10	4	7	35	26	2	6	13	18	40	34	21st

1951/52 First Division

42	8	6	7	34	32	4	1	16	15	56	31	20th

1950/51 First Division

42	10	5	6	28	19	3	9	9	22	40	40	13th

1949/50 First Division

42	10	4	7	27	28	1	8	12	18	47	34	19th

1948/49 First Division

42	14	3	4	43	24	2	6	13	23	44	41	11th

1947/48 First Division

42	9	5	7	29	23	5	5	11	12	32	38	15th

1946/47 First Division

42	14	5	2	52	21	10	2	9	38	32	55	4th

1938/39 First Division

42	13	6	2	50	25	4	6	11	21	43	46	7th

1937/38 First Division

42	10	7	4	42	21	3	5	13	16	38	38	17th

1936/37 First Division

42	12	6	3	52	27	3	6	12	20	30	42	10th

1935/36 First Division

42	13	3	5	35	24	7	4	10	22	33	47	4th

1934/35 First Division

42	12	5	4	46	20	6	1	14	25	50	42	10th

1933/34 First Division

42	11	5	5	33	19	4	6	11	25	52	41	12th

1932/33 Second Division

42	13	3	5	40	15	12	3	6	38	24	56	1st

1931/32 Second Division

42	14	6	1	47	19	5	8	8	22	29	52	3rd

		HOME					AWAY				
Pld	W	D	L	F	A	W	D	L	F	A	Pts	Pos

1930/31 Second Division

| 42 | 11 | 6 | 4 | 34 | 17 | 6 | 4 | 11 | 30 | 54 | 44 | 11th |

1929/30 Second Division

| 42 | 12 | 4 | 5 | 41 | 20 | 4 | 4 | 13 | 33 | 52 | 40 | 11th |

1928/29 Second Division

| 42 | 12 | 7 | 2 | 46 | 16 | 5 | 5 | 11 | 28 | 35 | 46 | 6th |

1927/28 Second Division

| 42 | 14 | 5 | 2 | 44 | 17 | 8 | 3 | 10 | 34 | 42 | 52 | 5th |

1926/27 Third Division (N)

| 42 | 17 | 3 | 1 | 57 | 11 | 0 | 6 | 5 | 35 | 29 | 63 | 1st |

1925/26 Second Division

| 42 | 8 | 5 | 8 | 32 | 23 | 4 | 3 | 14 | 22 | 54 | 32 | 21st |

1924/25 Second Division

| 42 | 7 | 8 | 6 | 22 | 17 | 5 | 3 | 13 | 12 | 29 | 35 | 20th |

1923/24 Second Division

| 42 | 9 | 11 | 1 | 27 | 10 | 5 | 7 | 9 | 17 | 32 | 46 | 6th |

1922/23 First Division

| 42 | 7 | 9 | 5 | 28 | 19 | 3 | 1 | 17 | 19 | 48 | 30 | 21st |

1921/22 Second Division

| 42 | 9 | 11 | 1 | 31 | 11 | 9 | 5 | 7 | 29 | 33 | 52 | 2nd |

1920/21 Second Division

| 42 | 9 | 5 | 7 | 26 | 16 | 3 | 6 | 12 | 20 | 40 | 35 | 20th |

1919/20 Second Division

| 42 | 13 | 3 | 5 | 37 | 15 | 5 | 3 | 13 | 23 | 42 | 42 | 10th |

1907/08 Second Division

| 38 | 11 | 5 | 3 | 43 | 13 | 5 | 0 | 14 | 14 | 39 | 37 | 10th |

1906/07 First Division

| 38 | 7 | 6 | 6 | 27 | 22 | 1 | 4 | 14 | 14 | 42 | 26 | 20th |

1905/06 First Division

| 38 | 12 | 5 | 2 | 41 | 15 | 4 | 2 | 13 | 13 | 40 | 39 | 10th |

	HOME					AWAY						
Pld	W	D	L	F	A	W	D	L	F	A	Pts	Pos
1904/05 First Division												
34	10	3	4	26	18	3	1	13	14	40	30	12th
1903/04 First Division												
34	9	2	6	45	26	1	5	11	9	31	27	16th
1902/03 First Division												
34	11	2	4	29	11	4	5	8	17	27	37	6th
1901/02 First Division												
34	10	4	3	31	12	1	5	11	14	31	32	6th
1900/01 First Division												
34	8	3	6	23	15	3	2	12	23	42	27	16th
1899/1900 First Division												
34	9	5	3	24	15	4	3	10	13	30	34	9th
1898/99 First Division												
34	10	4	3	29	17	3	3	11	18	35	33	12th
1897/98 First Division												
30	8	3	4	21	14	0	5	10	14	41	24	16th
1896/97 First Division												
30	8	3	4	30	18	3	0	12	18	41	25	13th
1895/96 First Division												
30	12	0	3	43	11	3	0	12	13	36	30	6th
1894/95 First Division												
30	7	3	5	35	25	2	3	10	15	42	24	14th
1893/94 First Division												
30	13	1	1	45	17	0	2	13	20	62	29	11th
1892/93 First Division												
30	8	2	5	33	16	4	3	8	25	32	29	7th
1891/92 Football League												
26	5	0	8	19	19	0	4	9	19	42	14	13th
1889/90 Football League												
22	2	3	6	18	20	1	1	9	9	49	10	12th